P9-CCY-097

What they're saying about

Today I Made a Difference

As a teacher myself, having worked with students from elementary through post-graduate levels, I have only the highest praise for *Today I Made a Difference*! Reading these stories from some of America's finest teachers made me extremely proud of my chosen career! Although I moved from the classroom through the ranks of administration, there is absolutely no doubt in my mind that it is the teacher who makes the difference in each student's life. This wonderful book captures those incredible moments when that difference becomes visible and tangible to teacher and students. As you read it, you will surely find yourself among the charming anecdotes, for each of us has been touched in some way by a special teacher in our lives. The authors truly epitomize the height of professionalism and humanitarianism—they bring Teacher/Astronaut Christa McAuliffe's words to life on every page: "I touch the future; I teach." I encourage you to take the time to settle down for a most enjoyable read!

Dr. Mary Ellen Freeley
Superintendent of Schools, Malverne, New York,
and Past President of the Association for
Supervision and Curriculum Development

Teaching is a job unlike any other. Teachers have the opportunity to change the world of each of their students—today and for their future. *Today I Made a Difference* captures the real difference teachers make in their students' lives. Through these stories, you see how teachers enable all children—those with disabilities, without disabilities, and with gifts and talents—to move beyond limitations and grow academically and personally. When you wonder why you chose teaching as a profession, this book reminds you how vital the work you do is to us all.

Lynda Van Kuren
Director of Communications,
Council for Exceptional Children

When I received the package from Dr. Underwood, I knew there would be many hours of reading required to thoroughly review the material enclosed. I must admit I did not have any specific expectations of what my review would yield; however, as I began to read each submission, I was enlightened, inspired, proud, and encouraged.

Each teacher and each classroom are unique, and as such, each must utilize different methods to achieve academic success. The diverse ideas and techniques perfected and executed by these most capable educators inspire me, and I hope will be shared to inspire their counterparts in other classrooms across America.

continued

I began my teaching career 35+ years ago knowing that a good academic education was and is the key that unlocks the door of possibilities for everyone. I am proud to see evidence that there are still gifted teachers who are dedicated to their profession and their students. Their experiences encourage me, and I am certain they encourage the communities in which they work, and affirm that effective instruction still exists and is thriving in our schools.

I salute these teachers, wholeheartedly applaud their efforts, and am grateful for the gifts and talent they share each school day.

Mrs. Elsie J. Rose
National Alliance of Black School Educators

I strongly support the publication of this book for many reasons. First and foremost, it is full of heartwarming stories of what is happening in classrooms all across the country. Secondly, it helps those who are not in the profession understand how truly dedicated teachers are today. Thirdly, it is inspirational to new teachers and those who are thinking of entering the profession. Lastly, it gives parents and community members an insight into how to work with our educators for the benefit of all children.

Anna M. Weselak
President National Parent Teacher Association

A Collection *of* Inspirational Stories *from* America's Top Educators ∾

EDITED BY JOSEPH W. UNDERWOOD, EdD, NBCT
Disney Teacher Award™ Honoree

adamsmedia
avon, massachusetts

Today I Made a Difference

Copyright © 2009 by Joseph W. Underwood
All rights reserved.
This book, or parts thereof, may not be reproduced in any
form without permission from the publisher; exceptions
are made for brief excerpts used in published reviews.

Published by
Adams Media, a division of F+W Media, Inc.
57 Littlefield Street, Avon, MA 02322. U.S.A.
www.adamsmedia.com

ISBN 10: 1-59869-834-6
ISBN 13: 978-1-59869-834-3

Printed in the United States of America.

J I H G F E D C B A

Library of Congress Cataloging-in-Publication Data
is available from the publisher.

This publication is designed to provide accurate and
authoritative information with regard to the subject matter
covered. It is sold with the understanding that the publisher
is not engaged in rendering legal, accounting, or other professional advice. If legal advice or other expert assistance is
required, the services of a competent professional person
should be sought.
—From a *Declaration of Principles* jointly adopted by
a Committee of the American Bar Association and a
Committee of Publishers and Associations

Many of the designations used by manufacturers and sell-
ers to distinguish their product are claimed as trademarks.
Where those designations appear in this book and Adams
Media was aware of a trademark claim, the designations
have been printed with initial capital letters.

Disney Teacher Awards ™ Program, Disney Teacher
of the Year ™, and Disney Outstanding Teacher ™
are trademarks of the Walt Disney Company.

This book is available at quantity discounts for bulk purchases.
For information, please call 1-800-289-0963.

*This book is dedicated
to the memory of
Bart Roen,
who positively impacted
teachers' lives
and helped make
their dreams come
to life
through the
camera's lens.*

Contents

PART I
Inspirations

PART II
Impressions

Acknowledgments

What began as a dream in 2004—becoming a member of an outstanding group of the best educators in America, meeting in Anaheim and Orlando and Anaheim (again) for unbelievable professional development sessions, and entertaining the outlandish idea of writing a book—has now become reality. We are all very proud to be a part of this work.

Of course, just like success in the classroom, success in getting our book from concept to fruition would not have been possible without the belief and assistance of many. We had several guiding lights at Disney, and Terry Wick certainly leads our Main Street parade. Patrick Davidson also inspired us to keep going. And, to our extreme delight, Art Linkletter is our "Star," as he has been for all of us our entire lives.

Thank you also to Dr. Meline Kevorkian and Jennifer Bayse Sander, who connected us with the right publisher, and, once there, Paula Munier, Brendan O'Neill, and editor Susan Reynolds for believing in our concept and helping us see it through. We would also like to thank the wonderful educational leaders who contributed positive feedback and helpful comments. We are very grateful to all of these outstanding educators and authors.

On a personal note, I would like to express my praise for all of my Disney Teacher Award Honorees who contributed to the moving stories contained herein. They make a difference every day, affecting so many lives in so many positive ways. This highly dedicated group of teachers helped me change my life a few years ago, and they continue to do so today. To my wife, Nancy, and daughter, Jolene, thanks for being so patient during the endless phone calls, ceaseless e-mails, and countless revisions. Thanks for the advice.

A Special Message

"A hundred years from today, the chances are that nobody will know what my bank account was, or the kind of house that I lived in, or the kind of car that I drove. But the world may be different because I was important in the life of a child."

After ninety-five years of an exciting, surprising, turbulent life, I'm convinced that, as John Lennon said: "Life is what happens to you while you're making other plans."

When you put these two thoughts together along with a number of true stories about educators who have inspired generations of young people to make this world what it is today, you have this book.

I have been a teacher all of my life. That may come as a surprise to people who think of me as an entertainer, a broadcaster, a businessman, a diplomat, a family man, or even as an ex-hobo who lived through the Great Depression hopping on trains across the nation while wondering what he was really going to be.

Today, even though I am lecturing at universities about how to become a success or writing about my adventures in Australia running a million-acre sheep ranch, or my unbelievable experiences in Africa, India, the Orient, and as a sailor in South America—not to mention my forty years in Hollywood as a TV and radio star, movie star, and now Regent of Pepperdine University and Chairman of the Board of UCLA's Center on Aging—I am honored to be asked to write this special message.

I love teachers. I am proud to be one. The future belongs to leaders now being taught by teachers to be lifelong learners. And, as a Disney Legend, I am pleased to be one of the sponsors of this great idea outlined in this book.

In 1930, surrounded by a world filled with unemployed people, I decided that I would go to a small, free college in San Diego and become a physical education teacher and basketball coach. It was a California teachers college . . . almost no tuition . . . almost no classrooms . . . and almost no students—fewer than 700!

A year later, astounded by all the other things that you could study, I changed to an English major and Psychology minor. I found I was good with words, loved to read, and got a big kick out of speaking. More importantly, I was "adopted" by an English teacher, a public-speaking teacher, and a psychologist. They were my first mentors, and their keen interest in my development played a strong part in my entire life. They inspired me to do more than I thought I could and I can never repay them for pushing me toward a career that I never could have dreamed of.

Now one of my chief lecture subjects is stressing the importance of mentors. And the second one I hit upon is attitude. In psychology, I learned that by changing the inner attitude of your mind, you can alter the outer aspects of your life. I also learned that things turn out the best for people who make the best of the way things turn out. This is covered in the book in the section titled "Interruptions." Because that is all problems and disappointments are. Don't quit!

I have already written more than I set out to, but I want to urge every would-be teacher to stay the course and win the future for our kids!

Foreword

BY DR. MARCIA TATE

Teachers are those who use themselves as bridges over which they invite their students to cross; then having facilitated their crossing, joyfully collapse, encouraging them to create bridges of their own.

—Nikos Kazantzakis

This book contains a collection of stories from some of the most worthy bridge builders in the teaching profession. Several years ago, I had the privilege of meeting one such bridge builder, Warren Phillips, who had been recognized as a 2004 Disney Teacher Award Honoree. He and approximately fifty teachers in Plymouth, Massachusetts, had signed up for a professional development class in which I offered twenty instructional strategies for engaging students' brains. I soon discovered I learned as much, or more, from them. Their passion for teaching led Warren and his classmates to positively change the lives of students every day. Fortunately, for the profession, Warren and twenty-seven other 2004 Disney Teacher Award Honorees bonded to share their life-changing stories. I congratulate them for their extraordinary honor and consider it a privilege to have been asked to write the foreword for their book. After reading their inspirational accounts, I am reminded of why I chose the teaching profession over thirty years ago.

There are three major reasons the educators who have contributed to this book are some of the top teachers in the world. Others would do well to emulate them. How do they do it?

They teach students first, and content second.

It has been said that rules without relationships equal rebellion. As you read the stories, one fact will become clear: These teachers take time to establish relationships with the diverse students placed in their charge. They appear committed to one common goal—helping students to achieve, even if that sometimes means unconditional acceptance.

They use brain-compatible strategies to deliver instruction.

For the last ten years, I have been working on synthesizing learning-style theory and brain research into twenty instructional strategies that take advantage of how brains learn best. In this collection, you will read about how these master teachers involve students' brains by having them actively engaged in meaningful discussions, project-based instruction, field trips, music, drawing, storytelling, games, humor, and other strategies that take advantage of how all brains learn best. These strategies bring the Disney magic into their classrooms.

They have a passion for what they do!

It has been said that the difference between an ordinary teacher and an extraordinary teacher is the moment where passion enters the picture. For those who do it well, teaching is not simply a profession; for them, teaching is a passion. With that passion, these teachers are making a difference in the lives of students.

Turn the page and feel the magic! Become enthralled with the inspirational stories of these Disney Teacher Award Honorees. Today and every day, they are making a true difference in the lives of students who are fortunate enough to cross their paths. I salute the twenty-eight bridge builders who shared their unforgettable stories in the following pages.

Dr. Marcia Tate is the former Executive Director of Professional Development for the DeKalb County School System, Decatur, Georgia. During her thirty-year career with the district, she was a classroom teacher, a reading specialist, a language arts coordinator, and a staff development director. In 2001, Dr. Tate received the Distinguished Staff Developer Award for the State of Georgia. Dr. Tate is currently a national educational consultant and has presented to over 150,000 administrators, teachers, parents, business, and community leaders throughout the United States.

Dr. Tate holds a bachelor's degree in Psychology and Elementary Education from Spelman College, a master of arts degree in Remedial Reading from the University of Michigan, an Educational Specialist degree from Georgia State University, and a doctorate in Educational Leadership from Clark Atlanta University. In 1994, Spelman College awarded her the Apple Award for excellence in the field of education.

Introduction

When people ask small children what they want to be when they grow up, teaching is rarely their top pick. Instead, they often proclaim a desire to become a firefighter, a doctor, a movie star, or a professional athlete. No one can blame them. Firefighters and doctors save lives, and movie stars and professional athletes are often famous and make a lot of money. It's no wonder that small children see little reason to become a teacher.

Most unfortunately, in this country, teaching is often considered a second-rate job. Everyone—even first graders—knows that one is not likely to become a millionaire teaching. Also, in today's political environment, the United States' educational system is neither respected nor praised. Today, the number of teachers within ten years of retirement far outnumber those pursuing careers in education. In fact, we may soon face a real crisis—not enough teachers to fill openings.

Research also reveals that the shortage of teachers may not stem from a shortage of new teachers to replace retirees; the larger shortage may result from teachers who have taught for two to five years and leave the profession. It's a sad fact that many of these teachers reach a point where they question whether teaching is the best career choice.

The temptation to seek another career causes us to lose talented teachers who could well become some of the best teachers in the profession. Every time we lose a great teacher from the profession due to retirement, or because business and industry lures them away, young people miss out on the chance to have their lives positively affected by a special person who might have made a significant difference in their lives.

During the summer of 2004, thanks to the Walt Disney Company, an elite group of teachers from across the country had magical, life-changing experiences when Disney selected them as National Honorees for the Disney Teacher Awards. When this group came together and began sharing stories, they soon discovered they were discussing the same issues and concerns, over and over, albeit in different ways.

Their conversations centered around two primary questions:

- Why teach?
- Why make teaching a career?

In answering those questions, they realized that collecting their stories might help potential teachers either join or remain in the profession. As such, the twenty-eight teachers Disney honored in 2004 constructed stories about their "Magical Moments" in the classroom. These stories illustrate the passion these teachers share for teaching and clearly illustrate that teaching is not a second-rate job, but is, in fact, an extremely important and rewarding way to live. *Today I Made a Difference* is divided into five sections: Inspiration, Impressions, Instructions, Interruptions, and Illuminations. The teacher-authors' fondest hope is that readers will feel inspired to make a difference in children's lives and become teachers.

A Principal's Perspective

DR. CAROLYN ADAMS

Southmoreland High School
Alverton, Pennsylvania

McDonald's Pennsylvania
Assistant Principal of the Year, 1997

The moment a teacher witnesses the look of understanding breaking through on the face of a pupil is simply magical. The magic of teaching, however, is conjured up without potions, spells, or wands. Learning, facilitated by an expert teacher, is hard work. That effort can be tedious, tiring, and frustrating, but for the person who has earned the title of teacher all pain is forgotten when the "aha moment" arrives. Teaching, the work that results in such magic, requires knowledge, skill, and passion. It is a profession that demands a commitment of unlimited time and unflagging spirit of those who undertake the job. Unfortunately, it is extremely difficult to calculate the positive impact of one well-taught lesson because its benefits are transmitted from peer to peer, generation to generation without an identifying tag. I'm not sure that my friends, children, grandchildren, or great-grandchildren will know or care that Mrs. Scott, my Advanced Placement English teacher, taught me to write. Her lessons will not be credited when a member of my family in the distant future writes an important book. No, her name will be lost; but her influence will continue.

There are so many unquantifiable factors in the teaching-learning process. Those elements, such as caring, charisma, and determination, when stirred together in the right proportions with the skills, knowledge, and passion of a well-trained teacher, constitute the magic. The expert teacher is constantly reviewing and revising her lessons. She factors everything that might affect a child, including the weather, into her equation for successful learning. And like an exceptional conjurer, her magical teaching will impact some differently than others. When in the presence of masterfully performed magic, we tend not to question the fact that the elephant disappeared, but rather ask how the elephant disappeared. Our next question in the sequence would logically be, "Whatever prompted you to become a magician?" Don't we want to ask the very same questions of expert teachers, the magicians who directly impact our daily lives?

The Disney Corporation understands magic. Disney creates magic through its motto, "Dreams really do come true." Adults and children alike are captivated by the magic of Disneyland, Disney World, and Disney Productions. Like teachers, Mickey Mouse as Merlin, Cinderella's Fairy Godmother, and Aladdin's Genie all help to make the impossible possible. It should come as no surprise, then, that the Disney Corporation has chosen to honor outstanding teaching with the Disney Teacher Awards.

As the principal and direct supervisor of a Disney Teacher Award Honoree, I was invited to attend a leadership seminar in Disney World that was a part of the learning opportunities offered by the Disney Corporation to each honoree. The thought behind the invitation was that any new ideas or programs gathered during the Disney Teacher Awards conference would require administrative support to be implemented. That sound reasoning brought me to Florida for a life-changing, magical experience.

Having arrived a little early for my formal participation, I had some time to myself before I encountered the 2004 Disney Teacher Award Honorees. Walking through the park, I couldn't help but think that the efforts of many great teachers were reflected in every aspect of the park. I wondered how crazy things would look if the names of the teachers who inspired or influenced the craftspeople were written on every item in the park. The place, I imagined, would be a mass of names. Art, literature, music, horticulture, engineering, mathematics, science, history, foreign languages, technology, psychology, and many other disciplines are represented in all that is Disney World. Behind each category are scores of great teachers. As I took in the wonders of the park and absorbed its energy and vibrancy, I was proud to be an educator. I walked taller, held my head higher, and breathed in a more rarefied air. But if I thought that the magic of Disney World was impressive, I was about to be confronted with an experience of greater impact. I was about to meet the multitalented, expressive, energetic, and ebullient Disney Teacher Award Honorees.

As a group they were a noisy movable feast of visual differences: tall, short, dark, light, men, and women. When I had the opportunity to get to know them as individuals and the honor to work among them on projects, I found them to be fiercely individual and absolutely committed to one common goal—helping children learn. Each has a story to tell that explains the magic and is worth reading. Each, like Houdini describing an impossible escape, will tell you how they make learning happen and what motivates them to continue to do so. Read the words they have written and then close your eyes while Mickey as Merlin waves his wand and fills you with the Disney magic of discovering mystical, wonderful, inspired teachers.

Today I Made a Difference

PART I
Inspirations

Everyone has a reason and a motivation for what they do. When times get tough, it is important to reflect and look back on these inspirations.

Why I Teach

HECTOR IBARRA, PHD

Middle School, Science
Iowa City, Iowa

I teach because I had a remarkable fourth-grade teacher; but to understand why she had such an impact on my life, you need to understand my life.

My mother had been an elementary school teacher in Mexico, and my father owned a grocery store. They used shopping visas to cross the border to Eagle Pass, Texas, to purchase items for the store. These travels soon prompted them to move us to the United States, where they believed their family would have more opportunities. After obtaining passports, we moved to Texas in 1955. A year later, because my mother was determined to distance us from the usual life of migrant workers and longed to finally settle in one place, we moved to Clear Lake, Iowa.

I started kindergarten that year, speaking only Spanish, and faced a world totally unfamiliar to me. My parents also only spoke Spanish, which made it difficult for the teachers and administration to discuss my learning needs with them. I was passed from grade to grade, not really learning anything. By the time I finished third grade, I still did not have a grasp of the English language. My older sister, Melva, had fared better, and served as the family translator. I relied on her to help me muddle through. However, tragedy struck that summer when Melva drowned in a boating accident.

I reluctantly began fourth grade, where I was introduced to Ms. Myrtle Olson, a teacher who would change my life forever. She had little time during class for individual attention, as she had a classroom of students who also needed to learn, but she saw something in me. She came to our house to speak with my mother to ask if I could stay after school to work on my English and schoolwork. I still do not understand how that conversation took place, as my mother did not speak English and Ms. Olson did not speak Spanish, but Ms. Olson had so much patience that my mother must have understood the meaning, or perhaps the sincerity, behind her words.

When I worked hard, Ms. Olson rewarded me with a friendly smile and a gentle touch. My alone time with her made me feel important. She made me feel like I was on equal footing with the other students and that I could be successful in school. She was tireless, identifying a variety of ways to address my learning needs. A petite woman, Ms. Olson had endless energy.

At home, my mother quizzed me with spelling words and helped me in math. Mother would often read, to the best of her ability, the questions I wrote for her to ask. As busy as she was, she never said no when I asked for help. I began to grasp the language, both written and verbal.

Thanks to my mother and Ms. Olson, I had learned enough English to be able to participate in a spelling bee! And I won! I won a beanie hat, something that wouldn't mean much today, but was priceless to me at the time, red propeller and all. Naturally, Ms. Olson was pleased with my progress and proud of my accomplishments.

Near the end of the fourth-grade year, I did not require as much focused tutoring, but we continued to focus on language and prepare for the fifth grade. We also had conversations that strayed to nonschool subjects. Of course, I realize now that these conversations were meant to help me practice speaking English, but at the time I felt happy that this special teacher took time to talk with me about my likes and dislikes, my family, my activities, and my dreams. I began to see a future beyond the school walls, and the walls of my family home.

Ms. Olson taught me the importance of hard work. She helped me believe in myself and helped me focus on the task at hand. She not only cared for me as a student, but as a person. Ms. Olson taught me that every teacher has the opportunity to make a huge difference in a student's life.

After fourth grade ended, I saw Ms. Olson occasionally, but I never fully expressed how much I appreciated everything she had done for me. It wasn't until my wife and I were expecting our first child that Ms. Olson and I really talked again. She came to our baby shower, and I finally thanked her profusely for the difference she had made in my life. After this, Ms. Olson and I wrote almost yearly letters to each other about what was going on in our lives. Of all of my teachers, she is the only one I have ever visited. When she died at age ninety-two, I was proud to be a member of her praying circle. Ms. Olson made a difference in my life and, I am sure, in the lives of many other children.

I became a teacher because I had a special fourth-grade teacher, and I wanted to be like her. Of course, I recognize that not all teachers can touch students the way Ms. Olson touched my life, but we are all awarded an amazing opportunity. When I teach, I look for opportunities to develop a lesson to better suit students' needs, to recognize the significance of interacting with students, and to provide an ongoing rapport to help them learn and feel good about themselves.

Learning extends beyond my science lessons, stretches across the curriculum, and goes outside the school walls. I create learning opportunities for students to see beyond the classroom so their imaginings can be part of their future, just as Ms. Olson helped me understand my imaginings could be my future.

Ms. Myrtle Olson was the most important teacher in my life, and she remains the inspiration for why I teach—for the moments yet to come, to open doors and create opportunities, and for dreams to become reality. I am proof of the impact one fourth-grade teacher had on a young student. I am proof that imaginings can shape your future. ∾

To Sir, With Love

WARREN PHILLIPS

Middle School, Science and TV Technology
Plymouth, Massachusetts

I still remember the first time I saw the movie *To Sir, With Love*.
I remember because watching Sidney Poitier portray a teacher
who made a huge difference in students' lives made me want
to be a teacher. I wanted to be brave and smart and principled,
someone who inspired students to break free of whatever obstacles lay in their paths.

I have been teaching seventh-grade science for over thirty-
three years, and each day presents a challenge. Students constantly test me with their crazy behavior, striving for my
attention, and consuming all the energy that I brought to school
with me on that particular day.

After school, I offer extra help to students, and then stay
even later to run off papers, clean the room, make sure students have fed the animals, watered the plants, etc. Then, I go
home and begin working on the next day's lessons, correcting
papers, filling out forms, and trying to devise ways to construct
creative learning techniques through interdisciplinary units,

songs, labs, and demonstrations. I am often tired and frequently overwhelmed.

The rewards are not always immediate. I remember a parent conference a few years ago with a mother and her daughter, Maggie. They were not happy about Maggie's science grade. I remember being very forthright with Maggie about her lack of effort and her untapped abilities—not an unusual lament at a seventh-grade conference!

"Maggie has the ability," I told her mother, "but she is not applying herself. She will have to work a lot harder if she wants to bring up her grades." I remember this conference because Maggie and her mother both cried, and I felt horrible.

The next day, Maggie came to me, "I'm going to try," she promised. "I'm going to try harder."

"Maggie," I replied, "Actions speak louder than words."

I asked Maggie to stay after school so I could help her with her science-fair project; she was floundering with a very simple experiment. After school, we talked about the importance of her experiment and the fact that her topic was really not scientifically significant because few people would care about the results of her work. Again, Maggie initially felt hurt, but, once again, wanted to do better. She began a new topic working with cranberries, an important topic because we have many cranberry bogs in the area. I asked her to call a local company and explain her experimental hypothesis to them. I worked with her on ideas about how to set up her experiment.

Maggie began working harder and stayed after school many nights. She eventually earned a place in the top-ten science-fair projects and continued on to a regional science fair. Each year I take my top-ten students on a trip to laboratories at the

Massachusetts Institute of Technology, and Maggie clamored to go and, when there, seemed particularly interested in watching real scientists in action. Afterward, she worked even harder and earned an "A" for the term. Apparently, we had successfully lit a fire under her, as Maggie proceeded to win regional and state science fairs in high school.

Years later, after a particularly frustrating and challenging day of teaching seventh grade, I received a letter from Maggie. Here's an excerpt:

> You taught me everything I ever need to know for the rest of my life. That is, to question. You set me on a quest for knowledge without me even realizing I was doing it, and I keep that drive with me to this day. One of the judges at the state fair said to me that I have the best understanding of the scientific method that he has seen. I told him that was because I had the best seventh-grade teacher in the world. He agreed. So thank you for showing and teaching me things more than atoms and photosynthesis . . . for lifelong lessons I will never forget.

Many of my former students are now parents and have requested their children be in my class. There is no greater compliment! It is also a great motivator. My new principal is a former student of mine who struggled in my seventh-grade class. Many of my former students are teachers, and three have contacted me to tell me that they are now middle school science teachers. I am a mentor for one who is teaching in my building. She stopped me in the hall one day and asked, "When does this get easier?"

"It doesn't," I replied, nodding sympathetically. "But real rewards do come . . . but are rarely immediate. Stick with it, and someday you'll see clear signs that it is worth the effort."

Today I have my students in class, and my former students as colleagues. It sometimes feels as if I spend more time teaching now than I ever have! Teaching requires emotions, and so does learning. I have strong feelings for my students present and my students past. Dealing with both of them is something I still love.

I haven't seen the movie *To Sir, With Love* in years. I haven't had time. But I still remember that teaching like Sidney Poitier was my goal; that I wanted to fully engage with my students and to make a lasting difference in their lives. Sometimes I know that I have, and sometimes I am very, very glad that I have another chance to get it right. When it comes to my teaching career, I like to parrot the students in *To Sir, With Love* when they bade farewell to Sidney Poitier: "Thank you, Sir!" ∾

An Unspoken Success Story

DARRELL WOODS

Hoover High School, Physics
North Canton, Ohio

After teaching high school physics for fifteen years, I knew well that time of the year—when almost every senior receives scholarship information at the last moment and needs a recommendation—never fails to arrive. I also knew that it inevitably coincided with weeks stacked to the rafters with challenges.

This week had been no exception. It had begun with a professional development day, filled with meetings and speakers on Monday; a science department meeting on Tuesday; a revised teaching schedule on Wednesday for a two-period senior class meeting; our monthly faculty meeting after school on Thursday; and our usual revised teaching schedule on Friday to allow a pep rally. To cap it off, I had agreed to stay after school on Friday to help students work on a special project.

And, as always, a stack of requests for scholarship recommendation letters lay on my desk. Thus, when I saw Stephanie breezing in with a letter in her hand, I knew what to expect.

"Mr. Woods," she said sweetly, "I know you are probably busy this weekend, but I just received information on two scholarships, and I really need you to write the recommendation letters for me."

I sighed and blew out a breath of air.

"I'm sure you already have a letter written from a previous recommendation that you can use by changing a few things," she said. "I really would appreciate it."

Again, I sighed.

"Puhleeze," she begged. "I'll have to pick them up before first period; everything has to be ready to go by Monday afternoon. Do you think you can do me this big favor, Mr. Woods, please, please?"

Despite the pile already destined to ruin my weekend, I always had trouble saying no to my students. "Sure, Stephanie, I think I can find the time this weekend to write them for you."

"Thanks, Mr. Woods," she said, bounding out of the room. "Have a great weekend!"

I sat down at my desk and surveyed the stack; obviously, my weekend was going to be spent working at my computer.

Moments later, Ruth, one of our guidance counselors, popped her head in. "Is this a bad time for a visit?" she inquired. She had the sort of Cheshire-cat look on her face that causes teachers to wonder: "What have I done now?"

Before I could answer, Ruth slid into a student's chair, leaned forward on her elbows, and whispered in a conspiratorial tone, "Have you found it yet?" Perplexed, I shook my head in the negative.

"I have been asked to make sure it hasn't gotten lost or misplaced," she said, offering no further explanation.

Completely baffled, I asked, "What? Have I found what?"

"When you find it, you'll understand," Ruth said, smiling. She then stood up and cheerily said, "Have a great weekend, Mr. Woods," as she dashed down the hallway and out of sight.

I carefully packed the folder containing the recommendation forms into my briefcase and began sorting the team assignment trays on my desk, searching for papers that needed to be graded that weekend. And then I saw *it*—an envelope with my name typed on the outside—in an assignment tray. I sat down and slit open the envelope. Peeking inside, I saw only one page, folded neatly. I tapped the envelope on my finger until the note slid out, and then slowly opened the page. It was an anonymous essay a former student had written as part of his or her college application about his or her "most exciting intellectual experience in high school." Here's a portion of what the unsigned letter revealed:

When I walked into my physics class, I was expecting to have a science class the same as all of the others. Thankfully, I was wrong. Mr. Woods was different from all other teachers that I had yet experienced. He moved a little quicker, figured things out a little faster, and actually held the class's full attention for fifty minutes a day. He accomplished this simply by making class fun. . . . Mr. Woods was a great teacher because he knew how to trick us into wanting to learn a little more, and then guiding us the rest of the way. The class was difficult, but I loved going to it every day. He inspires his students to search for understanding in their own ways, however unconventional those ways may be. Mr. Woods helped me learn how to turn "I think I can" to

"I know I can" and to accomplish it with eagerness, energy, confidence, integrity, and modesty.

Naturally, I felt flattered, but I also felt that warm feeling inside that many teachers long to feel and yet so often gloss over or forget. The essay reminded me how important it is to create a safe, diversified, and yet challenging learning environment. It reminded me that the real difference we make in our students' lives comes over the course of a year, every time we take an opportunity to light a fire under them or bring out something unique within each student. Our job is to make learning fun—and addictive—so our students will continue their education with vigor.

Ruth never revealed the identity of the student who wrote those kind words about me. I never had the opportunity to express my gratitude to this scholar or to tell him or her how much those words reminded me that my success as a teacher is not measured by awards or public recognition, but by the personal impact I have upon each individual student's life and his or her educational experiences.

Over the years, I have received cards chronicling the exploits of past physics scholars; pictures and e-mails updating me with interesting facts and current whereabouts of my scholars; and letters containing newspaper clippings about their personal lives and occupational advancements. Yet, among all these keepsakes and memories, I hold a very cherished place in my heart for the anonymous sender of that college essay. Its message has provided my soul with a special tranquility in times of chaos, and every time I read it I am reminded of what is most important and why I signed on to take on that responsibility—to make a positive difference in my students' lives. ⟳

Building Bridges

TAMMY HAGGERTY JONES

Elementary School, 3rd Grade
Sauk Village, Illinois

Students with special needs can create myriad emotional reactions. One of the best emotional reactions I have witnessed is the love and understanding that can blossom when knowing and working with these wonderful children. All you have to do is give them a chance.

In my school, our relationship with the Special Education Center (S.P.E.E.D.) began when some of my third-grade students found the unintelligible sounds made by six autistic children frightening as they walked through the corridors of our school. It was my first year at the school, and I was unaware that Miss Cyndi and her students had been renting space, in the farthest classroom, tucked away in a corner, isolated and alone, for the past five years. I was also a fairly new teacher, naïve about the educational and political changes that occurred in the state of Illinois during my five-year maternity leave, and a true believer of inclusion (although I didn't know it had a name at the time). To understand the full ramifications of this

15

dilemma, I put myself in the shoes of my eight-year-olds, as well as in the shoes of Miss Cyndi's students and parents. How could I introduce the children to each other and create a bridge of understanding, patience, and acceptance? I wanted to transform my students' fear of the unknown into positive relationships.

To begin building bridges, the children and I researched the various medical conditions: autism, fragile X, Angelman syndrome, seizure disorder, and cognitive delays. We then discussed them in the classroom, in age-appropriate language, as a community. We discussed the primitive developmental behaviors, verbal processing challenges, and constant adult supervision required in order to have the basic physical needs met. We talked about how each child was a person worthy of love and respect, and how each of us was created in a unique and special way. I discussed compassion with my students and created a safe place for them to express their concerns and grow. Within the first two weeks of school, my students learned the names of the children in the S.P.E.E.D.: Jessica, Austin, Aaron W., Aaron H., Dynver, and Nicole.

I had a small group of strong-willed children who caused disruption in my classroom, so I elected to send Teshyra, Markiesha, Wilbert, Lakim, Talmah, and Zachary to Miss Cyndi's room for fifteen minutes at a time. The idea was twofold: (1) to redirect the class's attention off the attention-seeking behavior and (2) to provide the attention-seeking children with a dignified "time-out." An added bonus occurred: Teshyra, Markiesha, Wilbert, Lakim, Talmah, and Zachary seemed to understand how disruptive behavior distracted everyone and would come back humble, quiet, and ready to join the class for instruction.

In September, I arranged for staff from the John G. Shedd Aquarium in Chicago to come to our school and present a "Voices from the Amazon" outreach program to 250 third-grade students in the gym. It was only natural to include the children from S.P.E.E.D. In anticipation of this event, two of my students, Daisy and Nakeyia, had read rainforest books to Jessica, Austin, Aaron W., and Nicole. Third graders Natalie, A'dreanna, and Jordan had assisted Miss Cyndi with art activities and offered to sit by Aaron H. and Dynver during the program. New friendships were emerging. Developmental differences were being replaced with childhood similarities. The grunting, humming, wailing, and tapping sounds made by the children in S.P.E.E.D. no longer frightened my students.

In October, my students were immersed in a thematic unit called, "Adventures from the *Book of Virtues*." I designed a character-development lesson, adapted from the children's book by William J. Bennett, around twelve animated PBS television videos. I was hoping that the selfless experiences in the S.P.E.E.D. Center and the new lesson would positively affect my classroom community. Miss Cyndi's students enjoyed watching the movies about Zach, Annie, Plato, Aristotle, Socrates, and Aurora. Together, the children glued pieces of orange yarn to the lions they were making after watching the story of friendship in *Androcles*. They added colorful feathers to the wings of Icarus and Daedalus while learning about self-discipline. Silver and gold glitter stuck to art paper, as well as to fingers, during *The Legend of the Big Dipper* lesson. At the end of four weeks, my students earned enough colorful and symbolic beads to create beautiful "virtue" bracelets and helped Miss Cyndi's students make bracelets of their own. The children displayed responsibility, courage, respect, honesty, perseverance, loyalty, work, faith, and integrity. Both classes proudly wore the bracelets long after the unit ended.

Slowly, friendships replaced fear. Eye contact, waves, and smiles occurred in the hallways. Miss Cyndi's students invited my class to their room for lunch, and vice versa. Children who hadn't visited Miss Cyndi's class wanted opportunities to read, help with occupational therapy exercises, and teach computer skills to Jessica and Nicole.

November's theme was called "Did You Ever Wonder?" My students read forty-three books, watched videos, and wrote essays about how some of their favorite products were made. We learned about ice cream, crayons, teddy bears, sneakers, chocolate, pencils, and cereal. Miss Cyndi's children helped us taste raisin, banana, rainbow, wheat, white, and cinnamon bread and bar graph their favorites. They joined us for a Bazooka Bubble Gum Blowing Contest, chomping, chewing, and giggling together while trying to blow the biggest, smallest, and longest-lasting bubbles. Our popcorn, chocolate, and ice cream lessons together were both tasty and fun filled.

In December, I received a grant from the Field Museum of Chicago to provide 250 third graders with the opportunity to experience the Soil Adventure Mobile, an outreach program designed to complement the museum's "Underground Adventure" exhibit. We invited Jessica, Austin, Aaron W., Aaron H., Dynver, and Nicole to join us. As the children rotated from center to center, excitement filled the air. At one station, Paco and Abel tested soil samples taken from our school. They compared the elements found in clay, sand, and black dirt. At another station, Autumn, Teshyra, and Willie were able to hold red wiggly worms, a centipede the size of a hot dog, and a very large African cockroach (eek!). The sensory experience was a thrill to behold.

That spring, a student of mine, Taylor, became the big sister to a brother born premature and with special needs. Taylor spent many days in class crying, fearing both the baby's possible death and what his life would be like if he survived. In total, four new babies were born that year, allowing the excited big brothers and sisters to share pictures with their classmates. To help Taylor feel more comfortable with her situation, Miss Cyndi and I worked together, giving Taylor extra time in the S.P.E.E.D. Center to see how children with special needs are cared for and taught. Gradually, Taylor's fears were replaced with love and acceptance. She brought in a picture of her baby brother and proudly walked the photo from table to table.

Our building-bridges experiment proved a major success. We all felt grateful, humble, and thankful to have met each other. Through shared experiences and frequent interaction, our community grew stronger and gentler. ∾

Who Will Save the Trees?

DANNY MAGRÁNS

High School, Humanities, Spanish
Clarksville, Tennessee

Every teacher experiences moments when he or she searches for a deeper reason to embrace the complexity of our profession. Why did I choose to teach? Why did I choose to teach Spanish at a high school in Tennessee, of all places? Do I still feel sufficient passion for teaching? Is it time to consider another profession? On those days when the answers seem vague or leave you questioning your choice to teach, a simple smile, a genuine hello, a kind act, a passing grade, a submitted homework assignment, or a thoughtful letter are all things that can turn the day around.

In 1991, while talking to some of my friends on the Tennessee campus of Austin Peay State University, a homeless man approached our group and asked for money. My friends said he was frequently on campus and knew him as George. George clearly had not bathed for a long time, slurred his words, and looked as if he lived on the streets. He appeared to be in his late fifties or early sixties. Based on these observations, I instantly presumed he was an alcoholic and refused his request for spare change, but our group offered to take him to a local restaurant for a meal. He refused.

Minutes later, George approached another group, who gave him a handful of change. George made a beeline to the nearest pub. A friend and I decided to follow him, to petition the bartender not to serve George, because, to us, he already appeared quite drunk. When we made our request, the bartender shook his head. "George never drinks," he said. "He comes in here to play the jukebox and uses whatever spare change he has to tip the waitresses for allowing him to stay and listen to the music."

Feeling seriously remiss in prejudging George, I took a seat next to him and engaged him in conversation. We talked about nothing in particular, but I wanted to know more about this man so I wouldn't be so hasty the next time. George did seem addled, and after a while repeated a set of questions that confused and frustrated me. "What about the trees? Who is going to save the trees? I need to save the trees," he said.

Eager to leave, I excused myself. George quickly followed and when we reached the street yelled, "I play the piano. I play the piano."

Something about him touched me. "That's great, George," I said, pausing. "I like to sing. Maybe one day we can get together, and I will sing while you play."

"How about tomorrow?" he asked. "Can we do it tomorrow?"

How could I refuse him? I scheduled to meet him at the Baptist Student Union (BSU) because I knew they had a piano. We made plans to meet at 1:00 P.M. the following afternoon.

As I walked home, I kept wondering why I had agreed to meet him. I didn't see a way that we could relate to each other or forge a friendship. We had nothing in common, really. Oh well, I thought, he probably won't show. And if he did, I could simply listen to his amateur pounding for ten minutes and then excuse myself. This wasn't too much to ask, was it?

The next day when I arrived at BSU, George was there, wearing the same clothes, hiding from a group of BSU leaders I did not recognize.

"George, why are you hiding?" I asked.

"Those people won't let me in," he said, fidgeting, looking distressed.

I suggested other places in the neighborhood, but each suggestion elicited the same response. "They won't let me in."

His feelings of being ostracized upset me. Since I was an Austin Peay student, I had access to the school facilities and had a right to bring guests along. "C'mon, George, you're with me," I said, holding open the door.

Once in the room, George excitedly offered to play hymns he had memorized as a young boy. I sat next to him for an hour in complete amazement. He was a talented pianist, and I was so moved by his passion for music and the sheer joy he derived in playing, that the experience brought tears to my eyes. I suddenly understood. George wasn't crying out for someone to save the trees; he was crying out for someone to save people—people like him. People who need love, compassion, attention, and help; people society rejects without knowing anything about them. George had shown his compassion by tipping the waitresses. He knew how to gain satisfaction within his circumstances, and because he could also see how much other people struggled in life, he gave to them first, understanding that if he didn't, then who would?

I spent the rest of the day with George, never quite knowing what to say. Mostly we sat together, shared a meal, and talked about nothing. I invited him to meet the next day, but this time he did not show, and I never saw him again. I did, however, often wonder about him and prayed that life had been good to him and that other people had opportunities to experience the same joy he brought into my life.

I gave George a few minutes of my time and he gifted me with the wisdom that only comes from someone who has been on both the receiving end and the giving end of charity. To George, I owe the wisdom that comes from a lifetime of giving back to others.

Though other experiences influenced my decision to teach, none impacted me as deeply as George's kindness on that beautiful fall evening. Regardless of our personal situations or status, we all have a need to give and to receive. In my situation, interaction with my students fulfills the need to give and to receive. I view my students as seeds entrusted to me. As such, I help plant, nourish, observe, prune, and shape the growth of their seeds. I do my best to teach them what George taught me: The best memories are those we create while serving the needs of others. But most importantly, I try to impart a feeling within each student that they are being seen, appreciated, and validated. I hope no student ever leaves my class asking, "Who will save me?"

Thanks George! ∾

The Second Most Important Job in Town

JASON M. LARISON

High School, Applied Fields–Agricultural Sciences
Holton, Kansas

I paced nervously in the corridor, awaiting my first interview. I was about to sit down with Mr. Buntin, a legend in the state of Kansas, a man who inspired me to choose Erie High School as my student teaching site. My nerves unleashed butterflies in my stomach as I entered the back of the classroom. Upon seeing me, Mr. Buntin peered over his bifocal glasses and continued teaching, never missing a beat. When a few students turned around and looked at me, I quickly slipped into a seat so I wouldn't disrupt the class. I was confident his students knew that doing so would have been foolish. When the bell rang, his students waited until Mr. Buntin wrapped up the discussion before rising, pushing in their chairs, placing their notebooks on the rack, and smoothly shuffling out the door to their next class.

After the students left, Mr. Buntin walked over and politely shook my hand. The handshake of that former Oklahoma farm boy was firm and powerful, and I would have expected nothing less. As we settled into seats in the classroom, Mr. Buntin skipped all of the usual small talk and immediately asked, "Mr. Larison, are you serious about teaching?"

I squirmed ever so slightly in my seat, took in a sharp breath, and answered, "Yes. Yes I am." And then, wanting to appear alert and attentive, I slid to the edge of my seat and sat up straight. Over his shoulder, I could see the photos of over 120 Erie seniors who had been awarded the State Future Farmers of America (FFA) Degree under his tutelage. The State FFA Degree is the highest award a state can bestow on a member, and no Agriculture Education teacher in the entire state of Kansas, probably in the entire nation, had ever had as many students receive an FFA Degree.

"If you are going to student-teach here you need to be serious about teaching," he said. "I don't have time to train bankers or feed salesmen. If you don't have a passion for teaching, this may not be the place for you."

I sat there wide-eyed, on the edge of my seat, wishing I knew how to impress this legendary man who had taught at the same school for thirty-two years. "I definitely want to be a teacher," I answered, meeting his eyes with a steady gaze.

"Well, Jason, I take my job very seriously. In my opinion, I have the second most important job in this town."

I looked at him quizzically.

"There are six or seven pastors and ministers in this town, and they have the most important job. They deal with a person's soul," he said, staring straight into my eyes, as if measuring the weight of my sincerity. "As teachers, we are entrusted with their minds, and that makes us a close second!"

• • •

Throughout my teaching career, I have reflected on Mr. Buntin's sage words and the lessons he instilled in me while under his tutelage. Although those lessons have manifested in different ways, the impact and importance of his deeds and his words still ring true. A student who entered my classroom as a relatively shy and nervous freshman is a perfect example.

Kim was an excellent student, but lacked confidence. Whether it was a classroom assignment or an outside-of-school FFA activity, Kim always welcomed a challenge, especially if it involved using her intelligence. Because she embraced challenges regularly, Kim constantly improved her abilities. By her sophomore year, she was the youngest member of the State Champion FFA Parliamentary Procedure Team that qualified for national competition. She had grown from a shy, nervous freshman into a confident young lady who battled whatever mental or physical challenges came her way. She was now part of a strong cohesive group. When her team stood in front of an audience of 2,000, she was nervous, but they emerged victorious, winning third place in the entire nation.

Over the next few years, I challenged Kim at every opportunity, and she consistently rose to the occasion. We learned to weld in the school shop, solve problems, and deliver speeches. Along the way, she absorbed as much as she could about the industry of agriculture. Still, when she approached me to share her career plans, I was surprised.

"Mr. Larison," she said, smiling, "I have decided to become an Ag teacher."

I was, frankly, thrilled. One of my brightest students would join the legion of students following in Mr. Buntin's footsteps, benefiting from his legacy.

Five years later, I visited Kim's agriculture classroom. As I slowly scanned her office, her desk, her classroom, and her agriculture mechanics shop, I saw flattering similarities to my own classroom—and to Mr. Buntin's. Our tour was interrupted when a young lady raised her hand and called out, "Mrs. Mitchell, I have a question."

Kim went over to see what she needed, and I stood there beaming like a proud father. It warmed my heart to realize that this would be only one of hundreds of students that will enter Kim's classroom in the coming years, one of many that would have the good fortune to study with an inspired and committed teacher.

Not all students entering my classroom bring Kim's level of intelligence, perseverance, and talent. Kim would have been successful in life no matter what she chose as a career. Kim was special, the kind of student teachers love to have in their class. But the best teachers feel a commitment to each of their students.

As teachers, we are expected to possess the skill and ability to nurture each of our students, regardless of their natural abilities or their financial or familial circumstances. Whether we are teaching a lesson in the classroom or guiding them as they work on an outside-of-class project or accompanying them on a class field trip or just listening when they want to talk, our task is to connect with each student and teach him or her something vital. As teachers, we sign on to accept the monumental task of challenging and developing their minds in a way that also opens their minds to all the possibilities that lie ahead. And, even more critically, we agree to seek ways to instill a level of confidence and belief in themselves that no one can take away. One of the most important aspects we must never lose sight of, as teachers, is the responsibility that comes with dealing with a student's mind. It is a huge and important responsibility. It is the second most important job in town. ∾

And Then There Was Allen

AIMEE YOUNG

High School, Humanities:
English, History, Holocaust Studies
Loudonville, Ohio

I had heard his name time and again, in the hallways and the teacher's lounge. Allen was one of those "difficult" students who had been labeled a troublemaker. When he was assigned to my sophomore English class, I decided to approach this young man in a way that would, hopefully, minimize problems.

Surprisingly, I found Allen intelligent, mature, sensitive, and personable. He was also an insecure and fragile young man, who was trying to find himself. He claimed to hate school and openly admitted that he couldn't wait to turn eighteen so he could drop out, as his parents and sister had done before him. In fact, Allen skipped school often. Still, I saw something in Allen that led me to reach out to him every time he attended class. I used every opportunity to stress that finishing high school was important, and slowly, my interest in him seemed to motivate him slightly—at least enough to pass sophomore English.

The next year, at the request of his eleventh-grade English teacher, I tutored Allen. Again, Allen made an effort and passed the course. Just before leaving for summer vacation, however, Allen came to see me. "I will turn eighteen in July," he explained, "so I won't be back next fall."

I was stunned. I had invested so much time and energy in hopes that he would change his mind. "Please, Allen," I said, "you've come this far. Please don't miss your senior year!" I had spent most of his junior year telling Allen that his senior year would not only be a lot of fun, but important to his future success. I had repeatedly urged him to finish high school and was not prepared to accept defeat.

"I hear you," he said. "Maybe you're right."

My hopes swelled.

"I'll think about it," he promised.

Summer came and went, and I had no idea if Allen would show up or not. The day before the new school year began, Allen showed up in my classroom, where he found me preparing for opening day. I was surprised—pleasantly—so much so I couldn't disguise my shock.

Allen smiled and said, "It's only one more year. . . . I can make it." I was elated! Unfortunately, the feeling didn't last long. Within the first few months, I could tell that I was losing whatever sway I held over Allen's choices. He limped along until Thanksgiving, but after the holiday break, Allen didn't return to school. Several of his friends came in to urge me to speak with him, that I was the only one who could change his mind.

So I called him. "Hey, Allen, it's Mrs. Young. What's going on?" I tried to remain cheerful and upbeat, but soon asked, "Are you coming back to school?"

"No," Allen answered somberly. "School doesn't matter. I'm just doing what everyone else in my family has always done. It's no big deal." Allen's entire family had dropped out of high school.

"Listen," I said. "Would you be willing to come over to the school to talk about this? I could set up a meeting with people who could help."

"How?" Allen asked.

"Well, I could arrange an intervention meeting to review your credits and figure out the best way for you to earn enough credits to graduate. Are you willing to at least meet with us long enough to review your situation?" I was virtually begging, but Allen was worth the time and energy.

Eventually, he agreed.

I sensed that Allen really wanted, deep down, to achieve what the other members of his family had not. Allen and I met with the intervention team to rearrange his schedule. We decided to enroll him in an Occupation Work Experience program so he could keep his job and attend school. I volunteered to tutor him in his other classes. To my delight, Allen agreed to the plan, and for almost six weeks, he attended school daily.

And then, Allen told me that he and his much younger girlfriend were going to become parents. At first, he tried to keep up with his coursework, but it wasn't long before Allen didn't show up for school for three days in a row. I tried repeatedly to contact him, by phone and through his friends, but I kept coming up empty, which matched the way I felt.

Admittedly, I was so disappointed I took it personally. I had gone to great lengths to "save" Allen, and I had failed. Despite my fondness for him and countless hours spent tutoring him, counseling him, and worrying about him, Allen fell through the cracks. I had used every motivational tactic I could imagine, even promising Allen a one-way airline ticket to anywhere in the world if he graduated from high school. Unfortunately, my offer wasn't enough to keep him in school. I felt so frustrated, and so deeply discouraged, that quite honestly, I found it hard to even think about investing so much in another student. I felt helpless, as if I had failed a student. And I also felt angry with Allen for giving up. None of these were pleasant feelings, and none were easily resolved. For a while, I withdrew. I actually gave up; I no longer believed that I could transform lives. This feeling slowly passed, but it took some time.

Then, one day—eight years later—Allen and I caught sight of each other in a grocery store parking lot. Allen greeted me warmly and told me he and his wife were expecting his third child and were moving back to town after living elsewhere for a few years. He didn't say much about high school, nor did he thank me for my efforts. My only solace came in recognizing that he respected me enough to greet me warmly after all that time.

Over time, I matured as a teacher and came to understand that I had, in fact, done everything within my power to help Allen, which is all any teacher can do. Over time, I restored my confidence and once again became more involved in my students' lives.

Yes, it's scary, and sometimes I question my penchant for trying so hard to positively intervene, especially when so many cards are stacked against me; but, ultimately, I worry more about the student and whether I *might be* the one who could make a real difference in that student's life, and so I make the effort. I have to. Those students are why I teach and why I work so hard for them. And they deserve no less. ❧

Taming Emely

JOE UNDERWOOD, EDD, NBCT

High School, Television Production and Moviemaking
Miami, Florida

Anyone who teaches for any length of time encounters a student who will change his or her life. As a high school teacher for over twenty years, I have undergone several of these transformations, and they are magical. In fact, it's my opinion that anyone who teaches will likely experience the following three truths:

- All students, regardless of what anyone says, can and will learn.
- You may not change the world, but you will change a student's world.
- You will have many students who will impact your life, and you theirs.

For teachers, these truths provide those much-desired magical moments. Just when you are ready to toss up your hands and concede defeat, an amazing young person will enter your classroom, challenge you, and re-energize your life. The feeling is unbeatable, but that student who gets under your skin and makes you grow may come with a caveat—they may be the son or daughter of a colleague.

Emely entered my class with that caveat. The daughter of a fellow teacher, Emely had a surprisingly negative attitude about learning. When she entered my TV production classroom as a ninth grader, she had a punk haircut and multiple body piercings. She immediately displayed rebelliousness and a lack of interest in education, which led to several informal conferences with her mother, all to no avail. I tried repeatedly to guide Emely toward using her frustrations in a creative manner, but she continued to rebel, driving her mother—and me—crazy. Our classroom conversations went something like this:

> ME: "Where is your video report on the new car called the Key West?"
>
> EMELY (SNARLING): "I didn't do it."
>
> ME (FRUSTRATED): "Why not?"
>
> EMELY: "Because I don't like cars, and I don't like the Keys."
>
> ME: "That's not the point. It's an assignment I asked you to fulfill—that your teacher asked you to fulfill—as part of your coursework."
>
> EMELY: "Whatever."
>
> ME: "Emely, the day you finally admit that you don't know it all is the day you begin to learn."
>
> EMELY: (A glowering, silent stare.)

Not long after, on a Friday night, I talked with Emely's mother at a coworker's wedding reception. Emely had been absent that day, so I casually mentioned it to her mother, inquiring whether she felt better. Her mother looked at me askance, "What do you mean? Emely's okay . . . as far as I know."

"Oh, great," I responded cheerfully. "Because she was absent today, I just presumed she was sick."

Emely's mother assured me that her daughter was fine, but she did not look pleased.

Monday morning, Emely returned to class in a sour mood. When we had an opportunity to talk privately, she confronted me. "Why," she demanded, "did you ask my mother if I was okay?"

"I was told you were sick, and it would have been impolite not to ask. Weren't you sick?"

Emely struck a defiant posture and admitted that she had cut my class, and then launched into a tirade. "Do you know what my mother did? She ripped my phone out of the wall, and she grounded me. I can't believe you ratted me out."

"Really?" I answered, nodding my head sympathetically. "How long are you grounded?"

Emely stared at me coldly, then sputtered, "Forever."

Rather than remaining sympathetic, I told Emely I considered this good news. "Now," I said cheerfully, "you'll be able to give your undivided attention to TV Production."

She grimaced, of course.

So I looked directly into her eyes and said, "Don't ever cut my class again."

Emely's mother had not grounded her forever, but actually being called on the carpet seemed to rattle Emely's own vision of herself (as someone who could be rebellious and get away with it). In ensuing weeks, Emely softened her rebellious attitude, and, over time, I was able to build trust and learn more about this complex and creative young lady. What I discovered was an underlying ambition: Emely wanted to produce our live daily newscast.

The daily newscast producer is my ultimate student-leadership position, normally held by a senior. As a producer, a student is not only in charge, he or she is responsible for everything that goes right and everything that goes wrong on the set, in our studio, and in the control room. I informed Emely that she would have to work hard to prove that she could fulfill these duties. I also made it clear to her that producers needed to earn the respect of their peers, whom they would be expected to lead.

Emely began showing up for class and putting genuine effort into her classwork and homework. As a result, she produced her first show late in her sophomore year, and performed well enough to impress me, and her fellow students. Although her mother and I had not yet completely tamed Emely, her fiery spirit, creativity, and spunk earned her classmates' respect. In truth, they may have feared her, but they also respected her intelligence, drive, and energy, and soon began going to her for consultation on their projects. Emely had found a way to channel her rebellion into thinking independently and readily expressing her ideas. The more her stature and confidence grew, the harder Emely worked. Eventually, she became an enthusiastic student who never cut another class.

On Senior Awards Assembly day, (a three-hour affair my students produce live on television), I strolled onto the stage and announced a special recognition. I generally presented our end-of-the-year recognition awards within our classroom/studio, and thus had never singled out a student at the Senior Awards Assembly. Nevertheless, I had been truly moved by Emely's trajectory and related her story—about a special student with a bad attitude and a worse approach to learning who had made tremendous strides in turning herself around.

Seconds later, when I announced her as my Student of the Year, Emely looked genuinely surprised, and embarrassed. Clad in a black TV crew T-shirt and jeans, with headphones still hanging around her tattooed neck, Emely emerged to accept her award. Emely's mother and I could not have been prouder. I had learned how to play it straight with a fellow teacher's child, and Emely had taught me how to motivate a rebellious student.

I'm happy to report that Emely majored in communications in college, where I'm told her untamed spirit and creative flair won her additional leadership positions. She is now in charge of digital media with an organization called Level 2, at the University of Central Florida. Now I call that a win! ∾

PART II
Impressions

One never knows just when that special student or

special friend will make a lifelong impact.

Payson

CLAUDE VALLE

Middle School, Math
Weston, Massachusetts

Payson entered my seventh-grade math classroom in September 1986, surrounded by a posse of boys at least a foot taller. Payson was not a great student, and in fact, he soon proved a terrible math student, but he was the leader of the pack—and a hemophiliac.

I had two goals for these kids: teach them math and help them be good people. Payson also had two goals: to be entertained and to do anything but math.

Payson was the type of student who loved asking teachers questions that would result in a story that would use up the rest of the period. He knew both what question to ask and when to ask it, so he was frequently successful. Plus, I was young, and allowed him to outwit me on many occasions. Over time, however, Payson found his ploy more challenging. He would then convince his friends to play distraction games, which meant I disciplined them while Payson leaned back in his chair, arms crossed, smiling. And if I let on that I was onto him, he'd extend both hands palm up, shrug, and say, "What?"

He drove me nuts, but somehow I liked him.

As fall turned into winter, Payson's multiple infractions were building, and my limited patience was dwindling. I often felt like this scrawny little twelve-year-old was running my classroom. He often left my head swimming with questions: "Why couldn't I reach him?" "Why didn't some of his peers tell him to cool it?" "What did they see in him that I didn't?"

Over the Christmas break, I had enough distance from the classroom to ponder my dilemma, and returned determined to toughen up and take charge. It was, after all, my classroom. That first morning back, however, I was called to an emergency team meeting that included all Payson's teachers. Several administrators ushered us into a rarely used conference room in a very hush-hush manner. Payson, we were told, the little boy who loved to disrupt, was now facing the biggest disruption of his life. "Payson," the administrator said somberly, "has been diagnosed with AIDS."

We looked at each other wordlessly. The administrator quickly told us that Payson had received a tainted blood transfusion and had accidentally been infected. This happened just months before testing of the blood supply became common practice. We were told that this must remain a secret, that no children were to be made aware of Payson's AIDS, and that we were not to discuss the issue with anyone outside the team. This was the first time the school was aware of having a student with AIDS, and the administration obviously wanted to proceed thoughtfully and carefully. We had been given our instructions, and almost as quickly as we were brought together, the bell rang and we were sent off to our classes.

I walked out into the hall, feeling absolutely stunned, my mind racing. In the 1980s, AIDS was a new and frightening medical condition, just beginning to be understood. Again, questions swirled in my brain: How would he handle this? Would he behave differently? Would he mellow out, be depressed? Might he be more challenging than ever? Would Payson know that I now knew about his AIDS? I walked into the classroom uncertain about what to do, and then I saw him sitting in the center of the back row with two henchmen on either side, and I knew nothing would fundamentally change.

Payson continued to run the show from the rear of the room, knowing exactly when to quit, but sapping every last ounce of my patience before he did so. In my mind, I continued to ineffectively manage Payson, and continued to grapple with finding a more effective way to deal with him. I quietly marveled at the way he seemed to enjoy my class, in his own way. He didn't seem depressed or frightened and, clearly, none of the other students knew his secret. Our interactions shifted. In an odd way, the more he misbehaved, the more my respect for him grew; and the more I let things ride, the less he pushed back. We were slowly moving toward a middle ground, an understanding. Whether it occurred by accident or design, I'm still not sure.

By the end of the school year, Payson and I had really connected, despite the fact he essentially failed my math course. This conundrum made me feel like I had failed as a teacher, but had succeeded in working with Payson as a person. On the last day of school, Payson thanked me and said I was his favorite teacher. "You always gave me a break and let me start over again fresh the next day."

Two years later, Payson and I crossed paths once again. He was a high school freshman and had joined the school's swim team—and I was the assistant coach. I welcomed Payson to the team and introduced him to his teammates. The other kids on the team had no knowledge, of course, of Payson's condition. When his bruises, due to hemophilia, became too pronounced, or his HIV treatments became too overwhelming, he stopped training. Certainly, this had to be frustrating for Payson, but he never let it show. He also seemed to be aware, though nothing was ever mentioned, that I knew about his battle with AIDS. "It's okay, Coach," he would say, "that's just the way it is."

Payson's condition never got in the way of any of his larger goals, be it disrupting a classroom, being part of a team, or respecting a teammate. There were times this 5' 6", 100-pound kid couldn't raise his arms above shoulder level, yet he'd jump in the water and outswim the other team's Goliath head-to-head to give us a victory. I finally saw the charisma in him that his peers could see years earlier. I also began to understand why kids followed his lead in the classroom—I witnessed his courage.

Charisma is something that can often be overlooked in a student. Or worse, it can be found to be frustrating. In my seventh-grade math classroom, Payson's live-for-the-moment approach led to incessant chitchat, inappropriate gags, and constant interruption. On the pool deck, his spontaneity surfaced as true excitement for the sport, enthusiasm for his team, and keeping loose under pressure. Through a different lens, Payson's negatives had become positives.

Interestingly, even though Payson's treatments were difficult and schoolwork was not his forte, I can only remember him missing one day of school. I'm sure there were a few others, but the one I remember occurred the day after Magic Johnson announced that he was HIV-positive. When Payson returned to class two days later, it was the only time he and I really spoke about AIDS. It was brief. He said he didn't need to hear about it all day—and that was Payson in a nutshell.

Payson went on to swim at the collegiate level and earned honors as an All-American, despite being almost a foot shorter than the next-smallest athlete. His college teammates learned to respect Payson's incredible heart as well. They, too, knew nothing of his battle with HIV.

Upon graduation, Abercrombie and Fitch (A&F) hired Payson, and in a few short years, he swam right up their corporate ladder. They marveled at his talents and had big plans for him. But just as Payson's world was expanding, he began to lose his battle. He had to leave A&F to move back home to Boston to be near the best hospitals.

Even at this low point, Payson continued to keep busy. He volunteered to help coach his old high school team, alongside his old high school coach. We all knew why he was back, but we did not speak of it. Anytime we dared to approach the subject, Payson would find a way to refocus the conversation on the tasks at hand. Payson found ways to inspire some of the swimmers that were struggling, and all the athletes respected him a great deal. And just like the rest, they had no knowledge of his secret fight.

Finally, in December of 2000, Payson lost his battle with AIDS, passing away at home after insisting he be allowed to leave the hospital. It was one week shy of Christmas. Payson was twenty-seven.

When news that Payson had died of AIDS surfaced, former classmates and friends were speechless. Each friend had respected Payson for his heart, charisma, and leadership, but now they admired and appreciated him in an entirely new dimension. Like me, they came to see Payson through a new lens, and their awe was palpable. We all recognized him as a courageous young man who never let his battle with AIDS interfere with his, or anyone else's, life.

Now, years later, I think of Payson often, typically when a kid is driving me crazy in class. Luckily, the memory conjures the lessons I learned from teaching and coaching Payson. What did I learn? First of all, if a kid is making me nuts, I've learned to ask myself, "Is there a way I can run things a little differently so that this kid's energy can be put to more positive use?" I've also learned that students have a shared history with each other that predates their classroom experience with me or any other teacher; and that I don't need to understand why to respect those relationships.

I've learned that, at the middle-school level, I only have my kids for three to four hours a week for ten months out of one year. There are a lot of other things going on in their lives and they bring these things with them into the classroom. Some kids are fighting battles I, thankfully, have never had to fight, but they are also learning lessons I may never learn—unless I am very attentive. Most of all, I've learned that patience, giving kids a break, and bending to work with them gets you a lot further than digging in and doing battle on every issue, every day. This is what I learned from Payson, and I'm very appreciative of what he taught me. ॐ

Yo Soy Maestra/*I Am a Teacher*

CAROL BOYER

Elementary, 5th Grade Literacy Specialist
Elma, Washington

When you are just starting out in the teaching business, you will generally take whatever position is offered. I was certainly no different. My introduction to my new profession occurred at a small country school, twenty miles from the nearest town. The school had an enrollment of 125 students, or so I was led to believe. I was hired to be the "Teacher of the Migrant Students." I wasn't exactly sure what that was, but I was told I would only have a small number of students, so I was willing to give it a go.

As the special projects director in charge of the migrant education program drove me to my new school, he pointed out the "sand dunes" piled here and there on the road, and the overturned railroad cars. "That happens when a big dust storm blows through," he explained. "Nothing to worry about really, just gets things kinda dusty." He explained how to keep my bearings in a brown landscape dotted with green alfalfa circles. What he did not explain (fully) was what I should expect in terms of the school, or how to make it work.

The school was located at a crossroads. My classroom consisted of a mobile home up on blocks, in a parking lot. It had apparently survived the dust storm, but not by much. The narrow trailer had not been used since the previous spring, so it was dusty outside, dirty inside, and full of broken furniture rejected by the rest of the staff. I spent my first weekend cleaning and salvaging the eight usable student desks and fourteen chairs that I planned to use for the reading and math areas. Even though we would be short on desks, the fourteen chairs would certainly be adequate for the small class I was expecting. Since most of the students were Spanish speaking, I decided the English-as-a-Second-Language area would be the floor, furnished with pillows and beanbags.

For materials, I received packages of scripted reading workbooks and two oral-language-teaching kits. No paper, pencils, scissors, glue, staplers, or tape were provided. My first foray into the main building's supply room was an eye opener, and a rude introduction to my coworkers. As I was calmly gathering supplies, someone approached, literally screaming, "What are you doing in here? You can't use these materials!"

It seemed I wasn't allowed to use the supplies, even if I replaced them later with special funds that had been budgeted for the migrant program. I soon discovered that my fellow teachers didn't consider me one of them, but a member of a group they called "those Mexicans." They viewed my arrival, and the impending arrival of my students, as a huge intrusion into the school's orderly life. In many teachers' eyes, my role during the school day was to keep the migrant students out of their classrooms for as long as possible. I clearly realized that I was on my own—in more ways than one.

So began my life of larceny. After leaving a door unlatched on a Friday afternoon, I returned on Sunday afternoon to sneak into the supply room to "borrow" enough supplies to make it through the first week. I walked out of the building with my coat and jeans bulging. I even had pencils shoved in my socks. (You can put a lot of pencils in your socks.)

Monday came and so did my new students, all sixteen of them. And I was about to get more. It seems the special projects director had neglected to tell me that the school population was about to explode. This occurred in my very first week, when migrant workers and their children arrived in pickup trucks and other assorted vehicles from Texas to harvest asparagus in a surrounding area. Virtually overnight, I had forty-five students who spoke only Spanish, and they had a twenty-one-year-old teacher with a shiny new teaching certificate and a dilapidated trailer.

Because the children couldn't pronounce my name, they called me *Maestra*. For the first few weeks, I struggled to teach normal lessons, but I quickly realized that I was learning more than they were. I was learning about discrimination and about school-system politics. I was learning about child-labor laws (and the blatant ignoring of them), about the value of education to better one's children, and about hospitality. I was learning to fall in love with my students.

Happily, my classroom soon became a haven for the students. They spoke Spanish without being made to feel foolish, asked questions about things they didn't understand, and felt free to be themselves. To breach our language barriers, we talked about everything: their migrant life, their fears, and their hopes for the future. I learned that one of my kindergarten students had polio, but still worked in the fields daily; that most of them got up at 4:00 A.M. to harvest asparagus with their families before cleaning up and coming to school; that two of my sixth graders were fourteen years old and would probably go to work full time after sixth grade; and that one girl would soon marry. Three of my students had been in the United States only three days, the time it took to drive from Texas to Washington. They had never seen an airplane, and didn't know that elephants really existed. They were afraid of the rushing water in the irrigation ditches. I soon learned that teaching English or reading or math was important, but that my job entailed so much more.

My job was to be there as a guide for students to discover this new world while maintaining a love and appreciation for their own rich culture and language. Yes, we read, wrote, and spoke English, and we computed math, but we also went outside to watch airplanes fly overhead. We learned to swim in a neighbor's pool, and we put on an assembly of folkloric dance and music for the entire school. I still regret we couldn't visit the zoo to see a real elephant.

Daily, my students showed me how much they cared about me. They brought me fresh asparagus and invited me to their homes. All of them lived in temporary housing. Some inhabited one- or two-room cabins with a single light bulb, with bunks built onto the walls; and some lived in mobile homes. I lived much like my students, in a travel trailer in the school secretary's front yard. A few growers provided homes complete with appliances, beds, and hot running water. Other families cooked with propane stoves and had only communal showers, restrooms, and water spigots. I marveled at how these students' mothers sent them to school each day in their Mexican school uniforms—brilliantly white starched shirts and blouses.

Although I was apprehensive about my home visits, their families always greeted me warmly. "*Por favor, maestra,* come in. *Nuestra casa es su casa.* Our house is your house."

One family offered me the only chair, served me coffee and cookies, and told me how honored they were that I visited their humble home. "Maestra, thanks to you for coming to our humble home," they would say.

I was the one who felt humbled, particularly when they described their difficult lives and how they came to the United States for the sake of their children's futures. They believed that education was the only way out of the migrant lifestyle, and they prayed daily that their children would not have to work in the fields as they did. They invited me to family parties, where I tasted roasted goat for the first time. They taught me "real-world" Spanish, while I taught them how to ask questions of the foremen at work. Often, parents studied right along with their children. We functioned like a team.

Thirty years later, I still remember the lessons they taught me: Stand up for your students and your beliefs; meet your students where they are, academically and emotionally; make parents your partners; form a community of learners; explore the world outside; don't take anything for granted; be grateful for what you have; and, if no other way exists, temporarily "borrow" a few pencils when your students need them.

What I remember most from those days is the affectionate way the parents and their children called me "Maestra." For them, the title relayed their respect and honor for the most important of professions, a profession that shapes the future of our country. Most teachers are addressed as "Mr." or "Ms.," but only a few are called "Maestra." I am proud to be one of them. ❧

Mission Possible

Elementary, Wellness and Sports, Physical Education
Delta Junction, Alaska

At some point in her career, every teacher encounters a very challenging student. I am an elementary physical education teacher, and my challenge was David.

When David arrived at our school at the age of twelve, he had never attended school. His parents had emigrated from a former Soviet Republic, which meant David spoke Russian. He had never learned to read and had yet to learn the English alphabet. His math skills were also very limited. David had been born with cerebral palsy, which affected his entire body and his speech. He was used to spending most of his day in a wheelchair, confined to his home, dependent upon others to move him when needed.

Teachers learned about David from his siblings, who were enrolled in our school. When they revealed that they had a disabled brother who spent his days at home in a wheelchair, the teachers consulted with the special education teacher to determine if we could integrate David into the school. Our school is in a small, remote community located at the end of the Alaska Highway. Nine months of the year, our ground is frozen and covered in snow. Most families that have children with such tremendous disabilities would not choose to live in such adverse conditions. Thus, we had never had a child in a wheelchair. We had also never serviced a student with cerebral palsy. Nevertheless, we wanted to try.

When his siblings conveyed this to his parents, they agreed to a trial period at school, and we assigned David to a combination class of fourth and fifth graders, under the tutelage of an energetic, caring teacher. In preparation for David's first day, our child study team met to determine how to accommodate his physical challenges and offer this child the best education possible. At one point, I asked when David would be arriving so I could also plan a curriculum. Everyone looked at me like I was crazy. They had just presumed David would not be able to join his classmates for physical education.

Luckily, I believed David and his classmates would both benefit from his participation in physical education. David would be able to learn social and language skills, and increase strength. The other students in the class would learn inclusive skills and how to modify activities for a physically challenged classmate. After much discussion, we all agreed upon a pilot program. "Quite frankly, Ms. Aillaud," the team leaders explained, "we have our reservations about allowing this child to participate in physical education, but we are willing to give you a chance."

I thanked the team profusely and reassured them that I would do my best to integrate David. "You won't regret it," I said, cheerfully.

David's father delivered my new student to his first day of school in a wheelchair that was rickety and dilapidated, a hand-push model that required David to depend on others to move him as little as an inch. Although David's arm movements were very limited, he was able to move his right hand in a relatively controlled manner. Our first goal became finding a way to give him as much independence as possible. The child study team immediately sought funding for an electric wheelchair that David could control. In the meantime, David became quite popular with the girls, who all clamored for the chance to wheel him around.

The school soon found a sponsor, who purchased David an electric wheelchair that he could navigate on his own, and David proved to be an ideal student. He soaked up knowledge like a sponge, as quickly and thoroughly as he could. He had a great sense of humor and an easygoing nature, both of which made it easy to have him in class. Buoyed by his new independence and an ability to interact with his peers, David became very eager to try everything!

In my class, I was determined to treat David like all the other students and to have his classmates accept him as an equal. I had little idea how daunting my goal would become. David loved participating in physical education class with all the other students, so we all worked together to develop modifications for him to join in. Whenever we ran laps, someone would push David's wheelchair for him (David was still a novice at working his new wheelchair and often needed assistance). At first, I cautioned them to go slowly, but they all protested. "How fun is that, Ms. A? David *wants* to go faster." They were right. David loved going faster and always responded exuberantly. He had never "run" before, and he loved it!

Together, we developed other ways for David to participate:

- During our hockey unit, we used duct tape to attach hockey stick blades to his front wheels. He still needed someone to push him, but he was able to score hits for his team. "Go, David!" they cheered.
- In the month of February, we conducted dog-sled racing in the gym. We didn't use dog teams. Some classmates served as the dog teams; others served as the mushers, those who "drove" the dogs. David became a musher.
- During our bowling unit, my husband and I constructed a cardboard ramp especially for David. He would instruct on the positioning of the ramp to best attempt a strike. When ready, he would bump the ramp with his right hand, sending the ball down the lane, hopefully on its way to a perfect score. "David just got a strike," someone would scream. "Hooooraaay!"
- When we played the parachute game, David was able to hold onto the soft cloth for most activities, but his favorite part was sliding under the multicolored material to experience the waves we created by shaking the parachute ferociously.
- Initially we tied the jump rope to his wheelchair so that David could participate. The more David participated; the more his strength improved. Over time, David became able to hold the end of a long jump rope and turn the rope. David also learned to "run through" a spinning rope.

David was anxious to attend our Jump Rope for Heart event, and worked even harder to acquire strength. All the students were given permission slips to take home so they could participate. Everyone brought one back, except David. When I asked why he didn't bring his permission form, he answered simply, "I forgot."

David's paraprofessional requested special permission for him to attend the Jump Rope for Heart event without his permission slip, but I had made a decision when he first came into my class that I would treat him like all the other students. "No," I said, "you're going to have to get permission, David." Everyone stared at me, as if I was being unfair. "If you want to participate, you can call home and get verbal permission from one of your parents."

Unfortunately, no one was home when he called. True to my word, as teachers must be, David was not allowed to participate. This decision was very difficult for me, but I strongly felt that making concessions for David would erode his sense of equality—and that his classmates might no longer accept him as an equal. The following year, David turned in his permission slip immediately, before anyone else. He had a great time twirling ropes for jumpers and "running through" spinning ropes.

By the second year in our school, David had surpassed all expectations of his academic capabilities, and he had grown tremendously in physical strength. His social skills continued to gain him the acceptance of his peers, and his confidence soared. As a fifth grader in his fourth/fifth combination class, he was participating even more during physical education.

David was even able to participate in our annual "Husky Hustle," a 3K cross-country race. Because we mostly have gravel roads in our rural area, this was not an easy task. David insisted on using his electric chair to compete, and to complete the race. I was a bit fearful and thought about insisting that he use his push wheelchair, but David was confident and determined that he could do it. We made an agreement that he could use his electric chair if he kept the speed down. When David crossed the finish line, the crowd cheered loudly. Afterward, I learned that David did keep the speed down, but ran into a large rock that nearly tipped his chair. Yikes!

As David progressed, his classmates accepted him as a team player. One day, I created a game called "Mission Impossible." The students entered to the theme song of the TV series and found an obstacle course. To complete their mission, they had to get their entire team across the gym floor without touching it. Equipment they could utilize in their quest had been scattered around the gym. They had to figure out, however, how to collect the equipment without touching the gym floor, and how to work cooperatively as a team. Our one exception: David's wheelchair would be able to touch the floor, but nothing else.

David's team wasn't sure how to use his abilities, until their ingenuity kicked in. As soon as David's team managed to collect a scooter and a rope, someone realized that they could tie a rope onto the wheelchair and David could use it to pull teammeates and equipment across the gym, through the obstacles, without anything else touching the gym floor. As David began his journey, his teammates worked their way cooperatively across the gym without touching the floor. As the competing teams edged closer and closer to the finish line, excitement mounted. When David's team crossed the line first, they all cheered loudly; and the minute the other team finished their mission impossible, they joined in the celebration. David's teammates were so pleased that David had helped them secure the number-one position; they circled him and gave him a loud "Hip, hip hooray!"

David always flashed a beautiful smile, but that day, his smile shone like a beacon. David experienced the pride that comes with accomplishment, and it was lovely to behold.

Some may say that I made a difference by including David with his classmates in physical education, but, in truth, David made the biggest difference. He taught me that with perseverance, determination, and a lot of creativity, almost any mission is possible! ∾

Today, I Was a Teacher

SALLY AUSTIN HUNDLEY

Middle School, Social Studies, Math, and Science
Waynesville, North Carolina

Because we have limited time with each student, middle school teachers are always looking for ways to provide power-packed morsels of learning in our content areas. In teaching math, I constantly worry about what will happen if a child leaves my classroom without deeply understanding the point-slope form of a line or how to solve for inequalities or how to fit a regression line to the trend of a scatter plot.

In fact, I was so concerned about my ability to teach them everything they needed to learn in a short amount of time that participating in a program called service-learning, which would pull them from the classroom to perform volunteer service work in the community, didn't seem like a good idea.

Nevertheless, we spent one morning a week going out into the community to help second graders improve their reading skills, to help volunteers streamline the flow of work in a neighborhood soup kitchen, and to lead crafts and exercise classes for the elderly. Of course, it was a worthwhile program; but I still worried about the loss of precious hours that could be spent learning math concepts.

After returning from our first trip out into the community, I asked the students to write about their experience and prompted them to answer the one central question that left me feeling conflicted: "Why," I asked, "is it important that we spend time with service-learning?"

Later that afternoon, one of the children's answers forever altered my idea of what was important in our schools. This wisdom came to me from Cassandra, a quiet, shy girl who never spoke above a whisper and never met my eyes when we had a conversation. She wrote:

Before today, I never understood why I was around. I wasn't important to anyone. I served no purpose. This morning, I talked with an eighty-three-year-old woman who couldn't leave her bed and who was lonely. She thanked me for coming to see her. Today, I learned that I can make a difference in someone's life. I do have a purpose.

Cassandra's words reminded me that the true purpose of education is to form and foster relationships: students with students, teachers with students (and vice versa), teachers with their colleagues, and each of us with our community. Nevertheless, I still worried about whether I had enough time to teach them the math concepts they needed to know. I wanted them to understand how to compute factorials and how to discover cube roots.

But service learning proceeded, and later in the year, Cassandra again impressed me greatly when she wrote:

> Today, I was important to someone. I hugged a child who was hurting. Today I made a difference in lives. I brought laughter to a child who was angry. Today I fulfilled my purpose. I brought hope to a child who was in despair. Today, I was a teacher.

When Cassandra stepped onto the stage at graduation, tears flowed on both sides. As we embraced, Cassandra whispered, "Thank you, Mrs. Hundley, for never giving up on me."

I pulled back to look at her. "Thank you, thank you, thank *you*, Cassandra, for teaching me what is truly important, for teaching me how to be a better teacher." ∾

The Power of Kindness

Elementary, Primary to 2nd Grade
Central Point, Oregon

A few years back, an inquisitive first-grade boy asked me a potent question: "What do you do for a job, Mr. Kuhlman?"

"Well, Christian," I replied with a smile, "I get paid to teach you."

"Really?" He asked, wide-eyed.

"Really," I assured the first-grader.

"Hmm, that doesn't make sense," he said.

I watched him patiently. I could tell he was mentally chewing on his next words. "I thought you did this just for fun."

Talking with Christian, as with many of my first- and second-grade students, always made me chuckle. He was full of more questions than I had answers. Many times our conversations ended with the class in a fit of belly laughs. Christian knew I loved to teach, and he knew that we had fun in class—a lot of fun in class.

Some of these fun activities included making flashlights and progressing through "astronaut training," with me as the

62

Mission Commander. Other classroom activities included creating penguin or dinosaur PowerPoint presentations; telling stories near our class-sized tipi (also known as a teepee), with me dressed as the Chief, complete with genuine buffalo headdress, and kids banging on drums they made in class. We also had fun with making fake kapok trees from the South American rainforests; making moving robots in an activity I learned from my mentor; making dinosaur fossils; pretending we were in Japan; incubating chicken eggs; and exploring the myriad stages of language arts, math, and writing activities. Regardless of what we were learning, kids had a "ton-o-fun" as part of the Kuhlman Crew. Even though I love to have fun, these activities are not why I teach. I used to think they would be, but that was before my first week of school as a new teacher in the fall of 2000.

When I first began my teaching career, I was assigned to first grade. I may have looked excited, but my wife saw terror in my eyes. Feeling complete shock and awe, I tried imagining how I could teach ones so young and new. I thought my skills were more aligned with teaching fourth- or fifth-grade students. Fortunately, the principal who hired me saw something different in me, and, luckily, he was right. But I didn't know that then.

I launched my first school year by inviting all the students I was lucky enough to have enrolled in my class and their parents to meet me, one-on-one, before school began. That way, the little ones could mentally and emotionally prepare for a smiling, 220-pound weightlifting man as their first-grade teacher. This seemed a brilliant idea, as every time a student walked through my doorway, my excitement grew.

One of the first students to arrive was a little boy that I'll call Phil. Phil was a quiet, withdrawn boy with blonde, tousled hair, a handsome smile, and a knack for frustrating his mother. During our conference, his mother warned me that Phil could be stubborn, didn't follow directions, and screamed if he didn't get his way, habits he had learned from her estranged husband, who happened to be Phil's not-so-kind father. She had left the man because of the way he treated Phil. I couldn't imagine that this little boy would be a problem in school. Phil seemed quite complacent at the meeting, but he was in a new environment. Time would tell if Phil's mother's warnings were to be proved prophetic or unwarranted.

School began and I was enthralled with my little class of geniuses. At the end of every lesson, I found myself thanking God I had become a teacher. As my curriculum began to unroll and my little ones began getting used to their routine, my confidence in my ability grew . . . except for Phil.

By the second week of school, Phil seemed intent upon challenging this new teacher to the limits of his patience. Even though I was having a fulfilling experience with twenty-one other six-year-olds, with Phil, each day was a new adventure in frustration. I kept plugging away, balancing efforts to keep Phil from disturbing the other students from learning with showing him the utmost kindness. I aged six months in that first week. I felt, rightly so, as if I was failing to reach this young man. By the second Tuesday of our time together, something happened which changed Phil for the rest of the school year, and changed me forever.

Phil was misbehaving during a math lesson using coins. He thought it was okay to grab the coins away from his math partner before she had a chance to solve the problem that he had apparently already solved. "Phil," I said, "treat your partner kindly, please." He ignored me and did it again, his voice rising in intensity.

Not wanting to embarrass Phil, nor draw any more attention to the situation, I walked over and whispered, "Phil, you need to calm down. Please move your warning card to yellow, apologize to your friend, and pay attention."

We used a colored card-pull system as warning cards. They all started with green. If a teacher issued a warning to stop a certain behavior, the child was instructed to move his or her green card to another color, such as yellow. If their behavior did not improve, then they were instructed to move their card to yet another color. With each card move, consequences rose. Of course, once a card was moved to warning colors, students had the opportunity to change their behavior and work their way back to the first color. Most of the time, it worked as a gentle reminder to follow the class rules.

With Phil, however, the warning card had become meaningless. Phil immediately became defiant, stomped his feet, threw his pencil at me, and began screaming at the child next to him, "This is your fault!"

"Phil!" I said, raising my voice a bit. "Your friend did not come to school today to be yelled at by you. Please, move your card, sit down, apologize to your friend, and pay attention."

Amazingly defiant for one so young, Phil stormed out of the room. After making sure he was fine, and within view, I let Phil cool off in the hallway until recess. I was actually relieved that I could teach without his distractions for a few moments. Soon after, the class rushed outside for recess, and I approached Phil, now sitting on the stairs outside our classroom. He had clearly been crying, but quickly hid his head in his arms.

"Phil, let's go back in and talk for a bit," I suggested. But when I reached down to offer him my hand, he flinched. "What's wrong?"

With a shaky little voice, and without looking up, Phil said, "I thought you were going to hit me."

I was horrified. "Why do you think I'd hit you?"

"I deserve to be hit for what I did."

"What did you do?" I asked.

To my amazement, and his, he couldn't even remember.

Since these were new waters for me, I simply repeated the class rules and the consequences for breaking those rules, and then asked him how we could avoid a repeat in the future. He stared at me with unblinking eyes, like I was talking in a different language and he was trying to translate what I was saying in his mind. "Are you going to spank me now?"

"No," I responded.

"Are you going to yell at me?"

"No."

"Are you going to push me around?"

"No."

"Are you going to make fun of me?"

"No."

"I guess you're going to tell my mom and tell her how stupid I am."

Again, I shook my head and said a sincere, "No."

Then Phil said something I will never forget. He raised his head, looked at me, and asked, in all sincerity, "Mr. Cool, are you normal?" (Mr. Cool was my students' nickname for me.)

Now it was my turn to look at him puzzled, blinking more than I normally would.

"A normal man would do all of those things; my dad would do all those things," he said.

I looked him in the eyes, put my hands on his shoulders, and whispered, "None of those things are 'normal' for anyone to do to someone else—especially a daddy to a son."

Phil sobbed and then thrust his arms around me, hugging so tightly he took my breath away.

Through tears he said, "I'm so glad you are not normal Mr. Cool." Then he let go of me as quickly as he had grabbed me, and went back into the classroom, and then to the playground.

I was eight days on the job and the reality of the responsibility I'd been entrusted with came crashing down on me like an avalanche. I noticed myself shaking and wasn't sure if the reason was my interaction with Phil or my feeling that I may not have been strong enough to carry out such a heavy responsibility. Slowly, the sound of laughter drew me back to reality. I looked down the steps and out the doorway windows at the kids playing outside. Despite the laughter and energy being expelled, I recognized that many of those children had boiling feelings below the surface; many of them had poor male role models, many were going through life with misconceptions about what constituted "normal" behavior.

I always knew how to have fun, and I thought I knew how to teach, but I wasn't sure how I could truly make a difference. I am not ashamed to say that, at that moment, I felt intense fear that I would fall short. I stood and walked into my classroom to wait for recess to end. Looking around the room at the small desks I realized how many kids I could positively influence in my career, and felt a bright future—for me and for them—unfolding in front of me. I looked at all of the little chairs, pencils, and nametags on the desks, artwork on the walls, and I smiled. Then I saw something that caused me to physically and mentally freeze in place: Phil had paused long enough to turn his warning card to yellow!

Phil taught me that some children might not expect kindness to emanate from an adult. As a teacher, we may be the first and only kind person they experience on a daily basis. There's a lot of power in kindness. It can change a life. It can change the world. I may not achieve perfection, but Phil taught me why I really teach: To change the world, one little heart at a time. ∾

15 and 1

JANEY LAYMAN

High School, Information Science and Business
Alverton, Pennsylvania

Sometimes, teaching is as much about the lessons learned in life as it is about the subject—in my case, high school information and business science. All teachers have an opportunity to share life lessons with students, sometimes on a daily basis. I have one life lesson I love to share with my students every year around football playoff time. In fact, I consider it such a powerful story and lesson I ask my students to write in their journals about the topic, so we can discuss it later. My lesson is called 15 and 1, and it begins with a list of 15 and 1 situations, as follows:

- 15 and 1: That illustrious record that NFL teams covet, yet few achieve.
- 15 and 1: A record that makes a team feel really great about themselves, almost invincible.
- 15 and 1: The regular season record of the 2004 Pittsburgh Steelers, predicted to be Super Bowl Champs, but

lost the AFL Championship when New England beat them in the playoffs. Game over. Season over.

- 15 and 1: It may get you to the playoffs but doesn't guarantee you'll win.
- 15 and 1: *Should* have been the best, but it wasn't. It goes to show that if you lose one playoff game, you're gone. Tough lesson, but a life lesson.

I teach my students that losing, defeat, and failure can be good things. A 15-and-1 record may or may not make you ready for tougher opponents. If it makes you humble, makes you try again, forces you to prepare better, and makes you think, then it's a good thing. If the Steelers had lost at least two more times, maybe New England wouldn't have been so hard to beat. Maybe that fifth Super Bowl would have been within reach.

I have a lot of students that reflect that 15-and-1 attitude. They're 15-and-1 when they leave high school, but when they reach college, they often face opponents who are 13-and-3.

Ah, 13-and-3, you say! Yeah, that's Adam, Jessica, and Kevin, your C, B, or A- students. And what's so great about them? They're not as likely to cop an attitude. They don't take classes to pad their resume or obtain a certain GPA. They're there for the right reasons. They've figured out that failure matters, that really learning the subject matters more than mastering test-taking. They've figured out that applying what they've learned to real-life situations matters more than a test grade. They've figured out that losing (or getting a B or C on a test) isn't necessarily bad; it's what you do with that loss (or test result) that counts. They've figured out that when they don't do well, it is best to find out why, and then work on improving that skill before trying again—and they always try again. They've figured out not only to keep persevering, but also to keep improving. They've figured out that they can learn how to handle something that's not so positive and turn it into something good. They're the students I want working for me.

I ran into one of those students right about the same time as the Steelers were kicking off their 2005 season. When I saw Kevin some years after he had been in my class, I saw how far he'd progressed from a young kid who wasn't always the popular one and who wasn't a top student. He had character, heart, and diligence. He was a student I would trust with anything. He would always try, and keep trying. If his computer program wouldn't run, he would keep tackling the problem until he got it to work. Kevin was a student who had to study to get a B, he was someone who picked his friends wisely and who didn't join clubs to beef up his resume or to get his picture in the yearbook. I knew Kevin would succeed, that he would graduate from college and make an employer proud.

Seeing Kevin reminded me of Adam and Jessica, both students who had tried more than anything to understand the "why" behind my every explanation. They had both loved doing projects, working as interns to other teachers, and helping other students as much as they could. Sometimes Adam and Jessica had to struggle to get the best grades, but they had both been jewels to those who worked with them. Both of them went on to work in the computer field, in management or programming positions, doing more than they ever could have hoped or dreamed. They also had integrity, desire, curiosity, and a thirst for knowledge. Kevin, Adam, and Jessica were all students with 13-and-3 records who'll win the Super Bowl of life, hands down.

As it turned out, the 2005 Steelers made it to Super Bowl XL, and they won in a fashion that no team before had ever done. Yes, there were other contenders, such as the 1985 Patriots and the 1980 Raiders, but the Steelers are, well, the Steelers. Those 2005 Steelers were the clear underdogs going in, gaining only a wildcard berth. They had to play every playoff game on the road. No NFL team had ever been the sixth seed to win a Super Bowl and gone on to win, but in 2005, the Steelers did. And by the way, they weren't 15-and-1 that year; they were 13-and-3. *That* is what I want my students to remember: 15-and-1 doesn't cut it, but 13-and-3 wins every time. ∿

Trevor

CASEY LaROSA

Middle School, 6th–8th Grade Social Studies
Montclair, New Jersey

I keep a worn, yellow folder in my desk drawer. Whenever I have a discouraging day or find myself doubting my purpose as a middle school social studies teacher, I retrieve it and flip through notes given to me by former students: Dominique, Rebecca, Minna, Jamel, Matt, and Julia, for example. Their expressions of gratitude serve as reminders that my decision to leave the business world—trading financial prosperity for making a difference in children's lives—was absolutely the right choice. Their heartfelt words nourish my spirit far more than money ever could. Sometimes, I'll jot down a success story and slip it into the yellow file, like those of Derek, Paul, Alicia, Mary, and so many others.

All those stories warm my heart, but the one that lifts my spirits most belongs to Trevor. Trevor has hemophilia, but if you met him, you wouldn't know it. His parents courageously raised him to be adventuresome—to live a full life without fear. Despite his physical vulnerability, they encouraged him to play

73

sports. Today, in high school, he plays lacrosse and hockey, and is both a guitarist and an honor student. When he first entered my sixth-grade classroom, however, Trevor appeared gloomy and morose.

Trevor knew from an early age that his condition had claimed the lives of many other children, including a few close to him. During hospital visits, he had often played with a family of boys—all older than him—who had become his role models. Each one had helped Trevor transition from one procedure to the next. Tragically, all three passed away from AIDS complications resulting from tainted blood transfusions. Trevor was four years old at the time, so his mom and dad had difficulty explaining their senseless deaths to him. No matter how often they reassured him that he was not going to die, Trevor was not convinced.

Luckily, by the time Trevor began receiving transfusions, hospitals tested blood for AIDS prior to transfusions. Trevor's mom and dad reassured him constantly that, while he faced a challenge in dealing with his illness, he would most likely have a very long life. Despite these reassurances, Trevor worried that he would die young. Although he was a bright student, he adopted a self-defeating attitude. "Why bother? I'm going to die anyway," he would say.

After meeting privately, his parents and I decided that a one-on-one conversation might help Trevor realize that we were all on his side. Not long after, I invited Trevor to eat lunch with me. After some small talk, we discussed the strides science had made in treating hemophilia. I reinforced his parents' message in relaying how blessed he was to benefit from new medicines, particularly preventive ones, such as the one he could take before a sporting event to minimize the risk, and an infusion he could use in the event he *did* get bruised or cut.

"My mom says that all the time," Trevor replied, "but every time I tell someone that I am a hemophiliac, they look at me like I'm already dead."

Trevor needed to hear that he was just a regular kid who was going to live a good life. How could I convince him that his hard work as a good student would not be wasted, whether he lived twenty years or ninety years? Unfortunately, no magic pill existed. As teachers, we do what the moment requires us to do, the best thing we know to do at the time, and hope for a positive outcome.

I wish I could say that my insight and care changed everything for Trevor, that he became the straight-A vibrant student that he is because of me, but that would not be true. I am also positive that I was not the sole reason Trevor began to see a future for himself. However, it is fair to say that we developed a relationship that began during his sixth-grade year, and grew during the three years I remained his social studies teacher. Over time, we learned to talk and joke around together, to respect and enjoy each other. When Trevor was in eighth grade, we even performed a rock song together in a student/faculty talent show.

Sometime during those three years, Trevor discovered that learning could be fun, and that he could enjoy sharing ideas. He eagerly soaked up concepts and grew to love history, government, and debating with his fellow classmates. If he needed to talk, we talked, but as he matured, the need for constant reassurance that hemophilia was not a death sentence lessened. My central role became taking advantage of any opportunity to tell him how much I admired his courage and his desire to make the most of his life.

After his eighth-grade graduation, Trevor continued to e-mail me from time to time, to let me know how things were going for him. We also occasionally met in person at the local coffee shop to talk about high school and history. During the time when the United States was deciding whether or not to become involved in the politics of another country, Trevor articulated his case—that it was our duty to do so—by comparing the current situation to that of Eastern Europe during the Holocaust. It didn't matter to him whether or not I agreed with his assessment; he had formed his opinion based on past learning and present facts and used his knowledge to prove a point. Most significantly, he truly cared about the people around him and about other nations. What more could a teacher ask for than to have a student who took the information she gave him and made it his own?

Not long ago, I encountered Trevor's parents at a local restaurant. As we engaged in polite conversation, I mentioned how proud I was that Trevor was doing so well in high school. His mom looked puzzled, and then emphatically said, "It's because of you."

I was so pleasantly stunned I could barely talk. How does one respond to such faith and admiration when it comes so unexpectedly? Knowing the feeling would be challenged again and again, that night, I wrote a postscript to Trevor's story and placed it in my yellow file.

I became a teacher because I consider it an honor to nurture and guide children. The responsibility can often feel daunting, and I am occasionally discouraged. I make mistakes, lose my patience, and occasionally fail to reach a student or inspire students to excel. Not all of my students will blossom, and I may never become one of the best teachers in the profession. Luckily, I don't measure my worth by fame or wealth. My reward lies inside the boundaries of the yellow file, where the words of former students, or their parents, tell me that I made a difference. So thank you, Dominique, Rebecca, Jamel, Minna, Matt, Julia, Derek, Paul, Alicia, Mary, . . . and, most especially, Trevor. ∾

PART III
Instructions

Instructional teaching methods come from a wide variety of places and are all unique. What is most important is not the textbook chosen or the technique used, but the lessons our students take with them.

Why Teach This?

AIMEE YOUNG

High School, Humanities: English, History, Holocaust Studies
Loudonville, Ohio

She raised her hand a bit timidly in my high school Holocaust Studies class. Her name was Kayla. I learned later that it required considerable nerve for her to finally raise her hand, not because she was intimidated by me, but because she was mentally preparing herself to argue with her teacher about a belief she strongly held and she was going to do so in front of the class.

"What are you going to do about it?" she asked.

"Perhaps sometimes it's best not to get involved," I replied.

"If you don't do something," she cajoled, "then aren't you helping it continue? Won't you be doing what you've been teaching us not to do?"

She was right. I had often lectured on the ramifications of hatred and the irresponsibility of those who refuse to get involved for fear of what might happen. But this situation seemed bigger than me, and honestly, not really about me.

In a recent school board meeting, a discussion had come up that was truly hard to believe. The superintendent had made a request to approve a field trip I was planning for my students to visit the Holocaust Museum in Washington, D.C. Incredibly, his request was met with comments rarely imagined in a school board meeting. A few unsavory ones included, "I'm tired of hearing about the damn Jews," "It's always about the Holocaust," and "I'm sick of kissing the Jews' asses." Shockingly, these remarks expressed the feelings of one particular school board member, who had voiced them at a public meeting!

Later that night, the superintendent called to let me know that my trip had ultimately been approved, but that there had been controversy. As he relayed what happened, I felt devastated, and admittedly, a little scared. For three years, after my Holocaust Fellowship trip to Poland and Israel had been publicized in the local papers, I had received my share of anonymous hate mail. Again, I felt as if I was being attacked, and I feared this type of battle, no matter the cause, no matter my views.

Seven years before, I had created and begun teaching a Holocaust course in this very small town of 2,900 for two simple reasons: The roots of prejudice still existed, and education was the best way to eliminate them. Nevertheless, blatant hatred came as a surprise. In this white, Christian, rural town of little diversity, it was startling to come face to face with such mean-spirited prejudice.

And now, one of my Holocaust students wanted to know what I was going to do to counteract the negativity expressed in the school board meeting. What *was* I going to do about this board member's show of ignorance? Would I choose to speak out or would I be intimidated into silence (as so many teachers are) because of this person's position?

I looked at my students, and then looked directly into Kayla's eyes. I promised them I would do something, although I had no idea what at the time. At the very least, I thought to myself, I could quietly and symbolically attend the next school board meeting.

And then, an amazing thing happened. A multitude of support arrived in a variety of ways. Letters of encouragement from community members poured in. Positive comments from former students appeared. Phone calls of appreciation from many others flooded the switchboard. The newspaper published letters to the editor criticizing the board member and praising my efforts.

At the subsequent school board meeting, people gathered in my defense. So many, in fact, the meeting had to be moved to the school's auditorium. During the public participation part of the meeting, over and over, parents, other teachers, community members, and students lined up to speak, asking for the board member's resignation or removal. They described what my class had meant to them, speaking eloquently and thoughtfully of education's ability to trump ignorance, praising me for opening up the world beyond the classroom, expressing disgust for the board member's remarks, and voicing the importance of learning about events like the Holocaust. Most of all, they stood in support of me.

It may not surprise you that these comments didn't faze that board member at all. Much like Mel Gibson did when spewing anti-Semitic slurs as he was being arrested for drunken driving, the board member brushed off his own anti-Semitic remarks with excuses of simply chalking them up to being angry (though his anger was directed toward another board member), and he refused to step down from the school board. At one point, the aberrant board member even tried to deflect the crowd's anger in my direction by saying that I was endangering their children by taking them to Washington, D.C., so quickly after 9/11.

Overwhelmed by many emotions, I could no longer just sit and listen. I had to speak. It wasn't what I believed in that worried me about confronting this man; it was that those pent-up emotions might cause me to say something I shouldn't. Luckily, the support shown by my students and community afforded me motivation and courage. Still, the walk toward that microphone was one of the longest walks I had ever taken.

Once there, I took a deep breath. "Sir, I am proud to say that you are the very reason that I teach my course. Ignorance like yours cannot be tolerated—particularly in education!"

When I left the board meeting that evening, I felt relief, and I felt good about what I had said. What had happened in that meeting had reaffirmed my reasons for teaching about the Holocaust.

We did take a group of students to D.C. that year, and we have done so at least three more times since. I have been teaching my Holocaust course for the last ten years to full sections of students, and I have had tremendous success as a teacher within the realm of Holocaust education. As a result, community organizations regularly invite me to make presentations relevant to the subject, and I regularly receive positive comments and calls from parents and others. The work that I have done, and the passion with which I do it, has resulted in my being named a regional educator with the U.S. Holocaust Memorial Museum.

The prejudice and resulting support that I found in those few months surrounding that long-ago school board meeting helped to shape me—and my teaching—in ways that nothing else ever has. The rationales I used to inspire my lessons really did exist; they weren't merely abstract ideals. Discussing this blatant ignorance, and the subsequent stance I took with my students, has caused much reflection on my part. The same students I influenced daily had taken on my role of encouraging, guiding, and questioning. They also trusted me to act. Now, more than ever, I believe in what and how I teach. I found support and faith among students and a community who stood by me when I was ready to simply let it quietly pass. What better example of lifelong learning could there be? ◌

The Greatest of These Is Love

SALLY AUSTIN HUNDLEY

Middle School, Social Studies, Math and Science
Waynesville, North Carolina

I am, by nature, a person of noise. Laughter, storytelling, fidgeting, and constant talking best define who I am, whether I am at home, with my friends, or in my middle school classroom. It is, therefore, profound that my most shaping moment was one of silence.

Not all children like school. This is a truism that most everyone can agree on. Regardless of their disdain for the classroom, however, it is always someone's job to teach them. I felt strongly that God had called me to work with children who not only did not like school, but who hated school. It was my job to figure out how to overcome this immense barrier.

I had spent a full year planning how school should run for those students not succeeding. I had convinced my principal to support a professional risk to throw out textbooks, teacher-made tests, and homework to meet the real needs of these at-risk eighth graders. Yet there I was, fully into the school year, experiencing overwhelming frustration. The excitement had died down and with it came the realization that these students were not only different, they were defiant. They threatened to kill teachers, openly cursed adults in their lives, became hostile with no explanation—and I had requested to work with them! These problems were shaking the core of my beliefs about students and learning, showing me how wrong I was about my planned program. With my heart and reputation on the line, I cried out one night, "God, you have placed me here and I am failing! How do I reach these children?"

The answer came back in stillness, with simplicity, and gave me peace, *You love them.*

Love can be a complex approach for the answer I was seeking. The answer did not imply that I should first give them discipline or that I should not worry primarily about their reading levels and their weaknesses. The answer wasn't about changing students; it was clearly about changing my heart. Love translated into accepting students as they were at that moment in time, while simultaneously holding a positive vision of who they would become. Love meant facing the day with the humor and patience these students desperately needed. Once that occurred, the other pieces fell into place. My conversation with God was one of the many paradoxes that I have witnessed since becoming a teacher of nontraditional learners. With love as my main goal, students have become more disciplined, more willing to accept traditional views on school and success, and more willing to accept disappointments without hostility.

At the end of the school year, we had traveled an amazing distance together. Through working with these students, I had become the teacher I desired to be. This journey, however, had one last challenge. Still facing us were the end-of-year tests required by our state. The students had gained so much, but these tests were the only measure that would prove their gains to the outside world. Some of these eighth graders had previously tested much lower than their current grade level, even as low as the first grade. Would they now, after all of our hard work, perform as students ready to enter high school?

With a twinkle of mischief in their eyes, the students came to the decision that they would happily prove their learning was where it was supposed to be on the tests. They made it clear that I had a part to play in this bargain, too.

"Oh, I don't know," I said with a bit of fear, "I don't know if I can do that."

"C'mon, Ms. Hundley, you have to. You just have to," they shouted.

My students outperformed even my expectations. Students who were chronically absent during their nine years of schooling had 100% attendance for the state tests. These students had the highest passing rate on the reading section in our school: 94% were on grade level in math and 97% on grade level in reading. They said they would prove themselves and they did. I was extremely proud of them, but they had not forgotten about our agreement. So, what was my part in the bargain? What was my part of, "You have to! You just have to!"?

I am marked for life because my students were successful. My ankle now permanently bears a tattoo. The students chose the ink that would decorate my skin. I was fortunate that they let me choose the design. My tattoo bridges the distance between us. It is in the shape of a stained glass image found in many churches. The three points of the triangle remind me to keep faith in the work that I do; to never abandon the hope that my work will transform the lives of my students, my community, and myself; and the greatest responsibility of my calling as a teacher. The one that was answered so many years ago by one simple phrase: The greatest of these is love. ❧

Two Toms

JULIE HARRIS

Elementary School: 4th and 5th Grade
San Diego, California

This is the story of two boys named Tom, a neat conceit since the name *Thomas* means "twin." The two Toms are not twins, but they did share a struggle as young students dismissed by the school system, although a generation apart. This struggle first inspired and then rekindled my passion to teach children at that golden age of childhood—grades four and five.

The first Tom is my youngest brother. My parents divorced when I was twelve years old and Tom was five. Each of us handled the breakup in a different way; Tom manifested all the emotion—the anger, the hurt, and the confusion. By the time he began fourth grade at our local parochial school, Tom regularly acted out in the classroom and on the schoolyard. He didn't listen, he didn't follow directions, he neglected his schoolwork, and he fought with kids during recess. His teacher attempted to gain control of the situation by making him sit apart from the other children in class, and allowing him to play alone on the schoolyard. The teacher even instructed Tom's peers to stay away from him, intoning that he was a bad influence on them.

Her words compounded my brother's stress. Tom walked our house at night, battling insomnia. His hair fell out, and he developed a skin rash. His behavior worsened, leading him to run away from his misery during school hours. The school would call my grandmother, who would troll the streets in her car, searching for him. My mother wrestled between honoring the school's authority and listening to maternal instincts to protect him. Finally, at the end of April, my mother decided to keep Tom home from school, to give him time to heal. It would take my mother's fierce love and determination, as well as the guidance of a fifth-grade public school teacher, Mrs. Stewart, to reverse Tom's cycle of fear and failure.

I was a junior in high school that year and already knew that I wanted to be a teacher. I'd always loved school and the challenge of learning new things. My passion was heightened by the heady smells of chalk dust, tempera paint, and sweaty bodies fresh in from recess. I was the kid who loved school so much she played school in her garage during summer vacation. So it was hard for me to understand what my brother Tom was going through. I knew he was difficult, hard to handle; I could see that from the way he acted at home. But I also knew that my youngest brother had many talents that went beyond the usual skills for school success: He could repair any neighbor kid's bicycle with ease and command a hefty fee that was gladly given. Tom became a successful entrepreneur in our community at the age of nine. Couldn't school provide an opportunity for kids like Tom as well as kids like me to experience success?

That year, I made a promise to myself: When I grew up, I would become the ideal teacher; no child in my class would ever feel the pain and humiliation that my brother experienced at the hands of his fourth-grade teacher. I vowed to learn how to help heal outcast students by employing love and compassion, rather than instilling failure by controlling them through fear and isolation.

The second Tom came to me thirty years after I made that promise. This Tom was an anomaly in my upscale suburban school. His father was in prison for drug possession; his mother was an alcoholic who often came to school in an inebriated rage; and his older brother had served time in Juvenile Hall. The family had been evicted numerous times. In first grade, Tom had been caught stealing food from the other children's lunches. He came to school in the same gray, oversized sweatshirt each day.

When this Tom walked into my classroom at the beginning of his fourth-grade year, I looked into his scared and angry and confused eyes and saw the eyes of my brother, the other Tom. I finally had a real opportunity to make good on my promise. I couldn't change what had happened to my brother in fourth grade, but I could make things right for this Tom.

Immediately, I faced a potent dilemma: How does one teacher summon the strength and wisdom to redirect a child who society has already pushed aside and would rather ignore? Firstly, I knew that this Tom needed a safe place, one that gave him a sense of trust, belonging, and significance. Since I only had one year to make a difference in his life, I met with my principal, Ms. Rens, and the special education teacher, Mr. Christensen, to establish priorities and enlist their help. My first goal became to increase Tom's attendance in school, so I struck a deal with Mr. Christensen to cover my class when Tom was absent so that Ms. Rens and I could go to Tom's house and bring him to school. Unfortunately, it didn't take long before we had to put our plan into action.

The first time we visited Tom's home, I knocked briskly on the front door, calling out with my most chipper Mary Poppins's voice, "Tom, it's Ms. Harris! I'm here to take you to school!"

Silence. No answer. Again I knocked, only this time a bit more assertively.

"Thomas, it's not right for the rest of us to have fun learning with you not there."

Again, no answer, but I could sense his presence behind the door and thought I could hear his measured breathing. I knocked again, and then pleaded with an even greater tone of authority, "Tom, at least open the door and let me talk with you face to face!"

I could feel myself growing increasingly tense and impatient. In my head, I could picture the rest of my class, wondering where I was, waiting for their day to finally begin. It wasn't fair that one student should consume so much of my time, attention, and emotional energy!

"You try for a while," I said, turning to Ms. Rens, who had been waiting patiently to serve as my backup. I was frustrated, but knew that we couldn't give up on him now; that would be too easy. It had been done before, to my brother. We had to persevere.

After almost an hour of tag-team cajoling, Tom finally emerged from his apartment. He remained sullen and silent, but he was out where I could see him and measure the impact of my words. We moved to a nearby stairwell, where I hugged him and whispered stories about all the exciting activities I'd planned for the day. The principal and I even made up a silly song to get him to laugh, to break down his wall of unwillingness. Eventually, we lured him to school. But the challenges of keeping Tom in school remained ever present.

Another day, another time, another absence, I was again outside his door.

"I'm not going without my new friend," Tom shouted defiantly. His "friend" was an eight-inch garter snake he'd found in a field over the weekend. He went back to his bedroom and returned with the garter snake housed in an old shoebox. Thinking on my feet, I told Tom that his "friend" couldn't come to class until our school secretary filled out the necessary paperwork to register the snake to attend our school. Somehow, Tom accepted my outlandish story. When we returned and I handed the shoebox containing the garter snake over to my trembling school secretary, I was thankful her dedication to children burned brighter than her famous fear of snakes.

Soon, our excursions to pull Tom from home to school became fewer and less necessary.

Once Tom attended school on a regular basis, I looked for other ways to remove the social barriers to his learning. Understanding that kids who play together well learn together well, during physical education class, I taught my students games that capitalized on cooperative teamwork, rather than athletic ability. We also held class meetings that focused the students on recognizing others' good deeds and progress by giving and receiving those compliments. At first, Tom sat on the sidelines, passive and silent, frowning like a disappointed Buddha, watching his peers and me interact. His classmates watched him, too, wondering when he would lose control and strike out against them as he'd done so many times in the past. As the teacher, I strove to model both how to reach out and connect and how to believe in the possibility of each other's goodness and success.

One day, during one of these class meetings, Paisley, a girl with a heart of gold, summoned courage to compliment Tom. "I noticed how hard you are trying to get your assignments done," she said. Like the crowd at a tennis match, the rest of the students' heads ping-ponged from Paisley, to me, and finally to the boy her classmates rarely acknowledged. Somewhat shocked, Tom covered his mouth, and then slowly nodded his head in thanks. Week after week, we'd all meet and talk, while Tom simply listened. Gradually, his trust grew, and he began to participate more and more with his peers.

It was an even bigger challenge to help Tom academically. Discovering that he had a wealth of information (from watching TV nonstop at home) to share in class discussions, I began to call on him more and more during lessons. Tom responded to this encouragement by making contributions about almost anything, from snakes to tsunamis, which added to the dialogue and showed his fellow students that he cared about contributing to the classroom learning.

Despite his wealth of information, due to his frequent absences and lack of support at home, Tom's reading, writing, and math skills were markedly below grade level. Recognizing that Tom's openness to learning was first and foremost dependent upon his sense of inclusion in the class, Mr. Christensen and I decided that we wanted Tom to stay in my class and not be pulled out for special instruction. We created parallel lessons for Tom that gave him the practice he needed at his learning level. This allowed him and the other students to see that he was working hard and that he was accomplishing something. I also discovered that Tom was quite an artist. Whenever we needed a picture drawn for a group project, whenever I needed an illustration during a lesson, Tom became our go-to guy. Eventually, he felt as if he finally belonged to the group, and realized that he had a stake in what happened that year. Bit by bit, Tom began to feel that he might succeed after all.

So, this is the story of the two boys named Tom and how they helped me become a better teacher. The first Tom, my brother, to whom I made my promise, still carries the scars of an unforgiving classroom. But he has beaten the odds, achieving great success as a businessman, and also as a wonderful father to his two daughters. My mother's unshakable faith and love provided the foundation, but a compassionate public school teacher named Mrs. Stewart, who welcomed Tom to her fifth-grade class, provided the model of acceptance I followed when my turn to make a difference in a student's life arrived.

The second Tom is still young, still has far to go, and still has many, many challenges to overcome. My prayer for him is that, in the brief time I had the privilege of being his teacher, he had a chance to feel, "If she thinks I'm worth something, maybe I am." ❧

Changing One's Views

DEB HURST

Elementary,
Kindergarten—English as a Second Language and Inclusion
Austin, Texas

Amanda was the most beautiful child I had ever seen, a real-life Goldilocks with beautiful ringlets framing her angelic face. Also incredibly bright, by eighteen months, Amanda spoke full sentences and soon amassed an impressive vocabulary. Unfortunately, on a frigid Super Bowl Sunday, Amanda developed a high fever.

Gut-wrenching hours later, after a battery of tests, Amanda's doctor delivered the life-changing diagnosis: Amanda had meningitis. Luckily, Amanda would survive, but she would also slowly lose her hearing, eventually becoming totally deaf.

Amanda's parents' perfect world came crashing down around them. Her mother, a former university cheerleader, and her father, a premed student, had to drastically change their lives. Instead of idyllically playing in the park with their beautiful toddler, they spent every opportunity seeking out audiologists, speech therapists, and schools for hearing-impaired children.

Amanda's advanced verbal skills began slipping slowly away, day by day, sinking her deeper into a world of total silence. When Amanda would frantically increase the volume on the television up to full blast and then shout, "TV broken," her heartbroken parents had no idea how to help. When her grandparents saw Amanda shake her baby doll and fling it on the floor when she could no longer hear it cry, they shuddered helplessly. Amanda grew so frustrated her tantrums were becoming part of everyday life. Their beautiful, bright, and happy child was rapidly becoming withdrawn and increasingly depressed.

Specialists recommended teaching Amanda speech to allow her the best opportunities for independent functioning and for learning how to read. These experts considered sign language a poor substitute for oral language development and discouraged Amanda's parents from taking that route. Her parents suddenly felt caught in an ongoing "Signing versus Oral" feud, when they desperately needed a way to communicate with their precious child.

When I became Amanda's teacher, the initial goal was to teach her to read lips and develop speech. But when three-year-old Amanda sat in the class circle, her bright eyes trained on me, I realized she was desperately searching for any clue to decipher what I was saying. At one point, Amanda jumped up, grabbed my face in her little hands, and shook it. In her frustration, she seemed to be saying, "Talk louder, doesn't your mouth work?"

Since I had never seen a three-year-old want to communicate as badly as Amanda clearly wanted to, I decided to do what was best for this child—to teach her sign language immediately.

Soon thereafter, sitting cross-legged on the floor, I held a baby doll and signed "doll" while saying the word.

Amanda quickly signed back, "doll" with a verbal "da."

Within minutes, we were patrolling the room together, signing "desk," "chair," "blackboard," "picture," "chalk"—literally everything we could identify and communicate. Amanda became a sponge, learning sign language faster than I could teach her. By the end of the day, Amanda could actually sign a few complete sentences.

In Amanda's case, Total Communication, a teaching method that included signing, lip reading, and speech, proved the ideal teaching style. The proof was in the pudding—Amanda adjusted quickly, becoming once again the happy child her mother and father missed so much. Amanda quickly picked up new vocabulary as well as speech reading.

Amanda became so excited about words and communication that she practiced sign language with everyone; she just didn't realize that not everyone else in the world signs. Her parents were particularly tickled when they found her down on her knees signing to their pet spaniel, "You want to go outside?"

Soon, we all got swept up in the process, and I began teaching sign language classes at night for Amanda's family and friends, meeting at the local pizza parlor, her parents' apartment clubhouse, or sometimes in the park. Amanda's parents learned to sign her bedtime stories, her cousins learned how to ask her to play, and her grandparents learned how to tell her, "I love you."

Amanda became a three-year-old rebel with a cause. When a stranger couldn't sign, she would place her tiny hands on theirs and literally shape their hands into letters and words, and, in doing so, this little girl launched her own private revolution. Each time I taught a class, a new friend of Amanda's would show up, recounting a story of how "that special little girl" had touched his or her life. Each was inspired by her beauty, giftedness, and tenacity.

"That Amanda is so beautiful," one of her friends said one day. "I bet she's going to grow up to be Miss Deaf America."

"That or the first deaf president," I answered, winking.

When Amanda's father was accepted to the Mayo Clinic to finish his studies the following year, I felt a sharp pang knowing I would never see Amanda again. But it was not her leaving that would stay with me; it was her arriving in my life that changed me, and how I would view each of my students forever.

Amanda taught me to stop asking, "*Why* am I teaching?" and switch to asking, "*How* am I teaching?" I began to question whether "tried-and-true" teaching methods, or even radical new theories, should be blindly accepted as the most effective way of teaching.

One rainy April afternoon, after a hectic day of teaching a bunch of bouncing kindergartners, I opened my mailbox and discovered a high school announcement. Out fell a wallet-sized picture of a beautiful girl—Amanda! Her hair had turned from golden locks to beautiful brunette waves, but I could still see the beautiful three-year-old I taught so many years ago. She added a handwritten letter about her busy life as an honor student and head cheerleader, and noted that she had been accepted to the University of Minnesota. Amanda shared that her hearing boyfriend was learning signs as fast as she had in my classroom, and added that she was in the running for Miss Deaf Minnesota.

Wiping away my tears, I read her final paragraph:

With graduation coming up, I got out all my class pictures from all my school years. My favorite was the memory book you made for me showing my classmates doing all the fun activities you worked so hard to plan for us. I laugh when I look at the curly haired girl wearing the huge hearing aids. Can that really be me? I have to admit, my mom and dad filled me in with most of the memories, but a mood comes over me that takes me back to when my ears closed and my world became a silent one. I can see you reaching out your hand; I can hear your hand. Watching your hands make pictures in the air opened the world back up to me. I just want you to know my world is a beautiful one and thank you for starting it.

Amanda had a hand in helping me become the best person and teacher I could be, and, if all goes well, maybe I will have the opportunity to cast my vote for Amanda as the first deaf president of the United States. ∽

PART IV
Interruptions

A teaching career is filled with challenges and

unexpected events. Success in teaching often depends

on how you deal with the little bumps in the road.

Trust the Old Man

JASON M. LARISON

High School, Applied Fields–Agricultural Sciences
Holton, Kansas

Whether you teach kindergarten, advanced placement physics, or high school agriculture, as I do, your personal stories and life experiences influence your teaching career. I was a high school junior when the day I will never forget happened, the day I knew my infallible high school agriculture teacher was wrong!

Mr. Carey had taught agriculture at Riverton High School in Southeast Kansas for twenty-nine years. Even though he taught an elective class, located in the old agriculture building across the street, the entire student body had elected him the "Most Popular Teacher" on numerous occasions. Most of his students were the sons and daughters of his former students, making him one of the most respected men in the community. Mr. Carey was an icon, an idol—my idol. But on that November day, I was convinced he made the wrong decision.

I belonged to the Future Farmers of America (FFA) group at school, where I held the office of reporter in the local FFA chapter. Mr. Carey served as our advisor. We had been preparing for weeks to compete in an FFA contest, our organization's first competition of the year. We studied hard for the information test. We had our parts memorized and we practiced, practiced, and practiced for our presentation. We practiced until we knew it forward and backward, until we had it nearly perfect. We boys from Riverton High were determined to make a name for ourselves.

When the day finally arrived, we were anxious and excited about the competition. We donned our blue jackets and ties before loading into the school's Chevy Suburban. As we pulled out of the parking lot, Mr. Carey suggested that we practice our presentation. "One more time might not be a bad idea," he said.

On the way, we stopped to grab some lunch. While we were in line ordering our burgers, somebody asked, "Where is Mr. Carey?" We looked outside just in time to see him in the parking lot emptying a bottle of liquid. Seconds later, he came in and asked Ben, one of my fellow FFA officers, to step outside. "The rest of you sit down and eat," he said.

Somewhat in shock, we sat down in silence, but soon began to put the pieces together. Clearly, Ben had stashed liquor in his book bag. Some of us had heard Ben mention in class that he might bring a flask of whiskey along—so he could have fun on the way home—but no one thought he was serious. It had to be a joke, right? Unfortunately, it was no joke.

After lunch, we resumed our trip, each dreading the consequences. Mr. Carey announced that he had decided to go ahead and take us to the competition. "I don't see a need to punish everyone because one of you made a poor decision."

By the time we arrived, we were distracted, of course, which meant we didn't perform at our best and didn't win any plaques.

The next day, instead of eating lunch, I stormed into Mr. Carey's office. My shock had turned to anger. I was furious at Ben. How could he have been so stupid? He had violated the FFA Code of Ethics, not to mention school policies. In my opinion, my friend's actions reflected poorly on our entire officer team. I wanted answers! I was barely through the door when I demanded to know: "What's going to happen? He is off the officer team, right?"

Mr. Carey asked me to sit down and relax. "Nothing has been decided yet," he replied calmly. "And, Jason, it's really not any of your business anyway."

"But you will strip him of his title, won't you?"

Mr. Carey sighed. "No, Jason, that's not the plan."

I seethed. "What do you mean he is still on the officer team? Mr. Carey, that's wrong." I then went into a whole rant about why Ben should be kicked off, how all the positive things we were striving to do had been damaged, but Mr. Carey cut me off in the middle of my debate by holding up his hand.

"You are probably right," he said somberly. "I may be wrong, but you are just going to have to trust this old man's instincts."

I shook my head, but I could tell he had, in fact, made up his mind. I was sure Mr. Carey was making the wrong decision, and I just didn't understand why or how he was choosing to let Ben off the hook so easily.

About eight years later, on a trip back home over Christmas vacation, I stopped by to see Mr. Carey. (I still visit him every time I get the chance.) Mr. Carey had been the teacher who motivated me to choose teaching as my career. He's retired now, and fondly refers to himself as "the old man," but his stories are even more interesting and possibly more meaningful, at least to me. During that Christmas visit, I asked Mr. Carey if he remembered that November day in his office. He acknowledged that he did. "I still don't understand why you gave Ben a second chance. Why didn't you kick him off the team?" I finished by stating clearly that I would have handled it differently.

My teacher studied me in silence. "There are a few things you did not know," he said. "Ben had been really struggling with school at the time. He liked agriculture and he liked being an officer in FFA. In fact, serving as an officer in FFA probably kept Ben at Riverton. If I had taken it away, I was fairly certain that he would have dropped out of school. Call it instinct; I had a strong feeling that I needed to keep him involved."

After I nodded my solemn agreement, Mr. Carey continued. "As a teacher you make hundreds of decisions every day. Some decisions are big and some are small; some will be right and some will be wrong. The best you can do is to always keep in mind what is best for your students and follow your gut instincts. If you trust yourself to keep in mind what is best for your students, and listen to your feelings, more of your decisions will be right than wrong."

Well, the old man was right, of course. But you would have to know what happened to Ben to know just how right he was. Ben completed his year as an FFA officer, during which he won some very notable state FFA awards. Ben did not drop out of school. He graduated. In fact, he was awarded a scholarship to judge livestock at a local community college, and, two years later, he transferred to Kansas State University. Ben became one of the few in our high school graduating class of fifty-four students who graduated from a major four-year university.

Every day teachers across the country make decisions that impact students' lives, and more than we like to admit, we don't always know the right decision. Sometimes the best we can do is trust the old man and listen to our instincts. ⌇

Where Were You...

PAM VAUGHAN

High School, Science
Camden Fairview High School, Camden, Arkansas

Sometimes, teachers experience a sort of déjà vu, as if they are looking at themselves through the mirror of time. All of a sudden, you are not a teacher standing in front of a class; you're a student sitting at a desk, looking expectantly toward the front of the room, wondering, "What's going to happen today?"

I had such an experience during my year teaching a high school physical science class in Fordyce, Arkansas. I had not thought about a certain teacher in years, but on that day, I felt as if I were again seated in her classroom, looking up at her with wide eyes, anxiously awaiting her every word.

The day had started like any other day, but I was admittedly nervous because I was new to teaching ninth-grade physical science. I had several years of experience, but after many years of teaching tenth-grade students, the fourteen- and fifteen-year-old ninth graders seemed very young. In fact, they seemed so much younger, I felt as if I were teaching in an elementary classroom.

I searched, planned, and developed what I hoped would be the perfect lessons.

The school was a small rural public school in a low socio-economic area of south Arkansas. My students and I lived the laid-back small-town life, where everyone knows everyone else and driving across town takes five minutes, or less. Our main source of communication transpired via word of mouth. We had greeted each other, taken roll, and were ready to plunge into our new lesson when someone knocked on the door. I glanced up to motion to the office monitor who picks up the absentee reports to enter, but it wasn't the office monitor . . . it was our librarian.

"Could I speak to you a moment," she asked, beckoning me to the hall.

I could tell by her expression that something was terribly wrong. As soon as I stood just outside the door, with my back toward the class, our conversation took a very serious tone. "A plane just crashed into the World Trade Center," she said somberly, "and something also happened at the Pentagon."

"Oh, my . . ." I said, stunned speechless. "What . . . what do you think happened?"

At that time, like most of the nation, no one knew what had happened beyond a few concrete facts. Still, we talked in hushed tones about whether the United States was being attacked, whether this meant that we were literally at war. Of course, we mentioned Pearl Harbor, the only other time America had been viciously attacked.

The librarian told me that she had been dispatched to inform the teachers of the situation. She had no instructions regarding whether or not, or how, we should inform our students. There was no procedure in place for such an event. As I watched her move down the hallway, I suddenly felt completely alone.

I had a classroom full of ninth-grade students waiting for me to re-enter the room, and I had gone far beyond my initial nervousness into completely uncharted territory. I had been teaching for seventeen years, but I had never had anything occur that approached this situation. What could I say to the children? Did I discuss it? Did I ignore it? Did I wait for administrative guidance? My mind was racing a mile a minute. And that's when my déjà vu moment occurred.

As I stared through the window at my students, I suddenly saw myself as a six-year-old girl staring at her frazzled teacher. I could still see her clearing her throat, smoothing her sweater with her hands, looking down briefly, and then choosing her words carefully. "Students," she said, "someone has shot our president. They have rushed President Kennedy to the hospital." We all gasped and stirred in our seats. "Let's have a moment of silence for President Kennedy, his family, and our nation," she said, bowing her head.

Not long after, a second knock on the door drew her out of the classroom once again. When she returned, she spoke even more softly. "Boys and girls, President Kennedy, our president, has died." I could see tears in her eyes, and remember being amazed that our teacher would not only feel such immediate sadness, but would allow us to see it.

As I stood in the hallway on 9/11, I remembered how my first-grade teacher spent a long time answering our questions—whether or not they made sense—quietly and honestly. I remembered feeling reassured when she shared her feelings with us, and feeling calmed by the fact she was not afraid to answer our questions, even if her response was that she did not know. Thoughts of that classroom, that teacher, and that day steadied me. I took a deep breath and re-entered the classroom.

As I looked into the innocent eyes of my students, who at that moment seemed much younger than their years, I felt a lump in my throat growing. I wanted to tell them as calmly as possible, but worried that this could be the first time they experienced this kind of hatred that could have led someone to crash into the World Trade Center. Nevertheless, I knew that I had to deliver the news, as calmly and cautiously as I could muster.

I found my strength that day in the memory of a teacher who had delivered devastating news to me thirty-seven years earlier. Lorraine Willis, my first grade teacher, not only taught me to read, write, add, and subtract; she taught me so much more. She made a profound difference in my life, and was still teaching me thirty-seven years later. Ms. Willis's greatness at one of the lowest times in the history of our country stands forever in my memory, and most especially in my heart. *She* made a difference. ॐ

It All Starts with a Dream

LIZ GALLEGO

High School, Dance
Dallas, Texas

I believe education begins in the heart. If parents fail to teach
their children the necessary emotional and social skills they
need to succeed in school, our heads may tell us that insur-
mountable obstacles may lie ahead, but our hearts tell us that all
they need is a dream to propel them forward. It's our challenge,
as teachers, to help our students find their dream. I have met
this challenge by creating a dance community in which students
have the opportunity to self-reflect, self-observe, and search for
ways to improve their skills, actions, and attitudes. By considering who they are being, what they are doing, and how they are
thinking—and then comparing their observations to who they
want to become—they expand their vision of themselves.

Sixteen years ago, a series of unforeseen events landed me in
Oak Cliff, Texas, a neighborhood considered a *barrio* in south-
west Dallas, where I have taught dance as a fine-art subject. Our
student population is rated 65 percent at-risk, and our school
faces all the challenges associated with urban schools. Our zip

code has the third-highest teen pregnancy and juvenile offender rates in Dallas County. We begin with about 1,000 freshmen, but since the school opened in August 1997, our largest graduation class had 442 graduates. Rather than looking for surface solutions or blaming teachers for these problems, I endeavor to steer my students in another direction, a direction that will fill their lives with something they had not known before.

As an experienced teacher, I know the precarious balance between curiosity and intimidation. In the barrio, learning needs to be real. If it's not real, my students see no value in it. So it's up to me to make what we do "real" for them. With carefully selected projects, I am able to motivate students to perform in public, participate in projects, and raise funds for costumes and travel expenses. Over time, I have been able to build meaningful and lasting relationships with them, and I am constantly amazed by the courage and determination they call forth to create a life. My students inspire me to find ways to make learning meaningful. My teaching has been shaped by the power of the arts and by the needs of my students. It's often a challenge to teach in the barrio, mostly because my students face cultural barriers where misconceptions are rife.

One former student named Roger was the first and only member of his family to attend college, but his cousins consider him a loser because he does not have a full-time job. He attends a community college and works part time for an acting and dance group called Junior Players, where he teaches dance at several schools, after regular classes have ended for the day. When Roger has a little time, he stops by and helps me tutor students and organize the costumes and wardrobe. Roger manages the family's meager funds and pays the family bills. He takes care of his grandparents, administering their medication and giving his grandmother her insulin injections. Every Friday, Roger spends the entire day cooking food that he and his mother will sell that evening to supplement the family income. Roger loves to teach dance. It is my hope that one day he can turn his talent into a full-time job so that his cousins will not consider him a failure. I am lucky to have Roger in my educational life.

Miguel has fallen asleep more than once on the studio floor, even with salsa and rap music blaring from the speakers. One might assume that he was out cruising all night with a gang or that he is lazy and does not care about school. In reality, Miguel works until 4:00 A.M. several nights a week, yet remains one of my most enthusiastic students. He is presently a junior, and I have hopes that he will be able to live the insane schedule that he has been keeping for just one more year. Miguel is not unlike many other barrio youngsters who go to school all day and then work all night to help their families. In fact, in some cases, students like Miguel are the sole breadwinners for their entire family. Because our class provides increased personal interaction, I learned of Miguel's overnight work, which allows me to understand his situation and help him as much as I can.

Nereyda is a single mom and an honor student. She recently fainted between classes. Eager to catch up on her studies after returning from having the baby, in order to graduate on time, Nereyda was devoting every minute to studying and caring for her newborn child. Working around the clock without much sleep and without proper nourishment, she soon collapsed. The school nurse was able to assist her in obtaining social services. Despite her challenges, Nereyda exudes a pleasant, cheerful disposition and is determined to graduate. She told me after returning to school, "I don't think I would have come back if it weren't for this class."

Martin, an illegal immigrant, came to the United States at the beginning of his freshman year. Because of his limited English proficiency, he began high school at the Language Academy, but at the end of that year, the school placed him in regular classes. Martin worked hard to learn English, he worked hard on his academic classes, and he worked hard in my classes. Martin worked so hard he completed eight advanced placement courses during his senior year and still graduated as valedictorian of his class. The power for his superhuman achievement came from a *relicario*, a diadem, he carried in his backpack that reminded him of the pledge he made to his grandfather to do his best. Martin selected *folklórico* dance as an elective because he was homesick for his native Monterey. Today, he is pursuing a career in education.

Evelyn came to me as a very shy girl. Her Spanish-speaking mother was convinced that her shyness would prevent her from succeeding in the world. During her four years in the dance program, Evelyn's metamorphosis from a visibly trembling to a radiantly confident young woman was something to behold. Evelyn's shyness was matched with an iron will. At the end of her freshman year, she tried out for baton twirler with the marching band. During her junior year, she tried out for the girls' softball team. Evelyn graduated in the top 10 percent of her class. Today, she is in college studying zoology with the hopes of becoming a veterinarian specializing in reptiles.

Karla was so inspired by my dance program she has literally followed in my footsteps, majoring in dance education at my old alma mater. I have been inspired by Karla's tenacity to cling to her dream in the face of the setbacks. Karla, an immigrant and an honors graduate, enrolled in community college one semester before the Noriega Act was passed, making her ineligible for any of its benefits. It has taken her a long time to work her way through school as an international student. After seven years of holding steadfast, she is finally a senior attending college full time. Karla is currently planning her second presentation for the National Dance Association Annual Conference.

Not all the students who inspire me are honor students. Larry was a special education student who was left to fend for himself when his mother's common-law husband died, leaving them without benefits or income, and his mother moved in with relatives in Oklahoma. Every year, during the Texas State Fair, Larry slept on the dance-studio floor, exhausted from having worked at the fair late into the night. I will never forget his determination to graduate, and the triumph of his success.

Lizbeth, a shy special education student with remarkable dance ability, created a priceless experience for both of us. When she was absent for two weeks, I called her home. Her mom explained that she was recovering from jaw surgery, and then said, "I can't thank you enough for the happiness you have given my daughter. Dance is all she talks about."

Unfortunately, some of my students do drop out of school. This is a great loss not only to the individual students, but also to our communities, our nation, and to humanity. As a teacher, I ask myself what is needed for something different to occur. In looking at the success of many of my dance students, it becomes increasingly clear that they had the vision to create a dream and somehow manifest the courage. Having a sense of purpose and a belief that they could achieve their dreams made all the difference.

Agnes de Mille once said, "To dance is to be out of yourself ... larger, more powerful, more beautiful. This is power. It is glory on earth, and it is yours for the taking."

I use the power of dance to empower confidence and self-esteem in hopes of creating the fertile ground where a dream might grow. All students deserve an education that begins with a dream. Each day, I do my best to light a fire in each student's soul, assist them in developing a sense of purpose, encourage them to experience the joy in the moment and in awakening self-knowledge. Each day, I teach. ∾

Plain Walls to Plane Walls

DARLENE MARTIN

High School, Math
Grafton, West Virginia

A train leaves New York City at 1:00 P.M. heading for Chicago, traveling at eighty-five miles per hour. Another train leaves Chicago heading for New York City at 6:00 P.M., traveling at seventy miles per hour. At what time do they meet?

This scenario has triggered anxiety that has prevented many students from enjoying the study of mathematics. To prevent students from shying away from mathematics, rather than creating word problems or problems that required calculations, I created a mathematical experience for my high school students. Instead of lesson plans following the same track (pardon the pun) every year, I realized that the best journey I can offer my students involves changing direction occasionally and going on some incredible, implausible mathematical side trips.

The first part of their trip begins at the station: my classroom. "Plain Walls to Plane Walls" is a project I have used to define my classroom environment since 1991. When I first embarked on my teaching career, I used a cardboard box to introduce and illustrate the various concepts of points, lines, and planes. One day it occurred to me: The classroom could illustrate the box, and we could be inside the model (something like the Disney movie *Honey, I Shrunk the Kids!*). I then painted each of the walls in my classroom a different color. This approach made it simple to refer to the various planes: the pink plane, the blue plane, and so on. I placed tape at the corners of the room to illustrate how two planes intersect to create a line. Ping-pong balls suspended with fishing line became our points. From the students' desks, the points appeared to be suspended in midair. Two retractable clotheslines stretched across the room to illustrate intersecting, parallel, and skew lines. Colorful magnetic letters identified named points on the metal walls, and clothespins marked points on the lines. This thought-provoking activity still motivates my students the moment they enter the classroom.

Instead of being greeted by four plain walls, they see four "plane" walls, and discussion begins immediately. Immersing the students in a geometric model constantly reminds them what we are studying. Each August we gather at the station (remember, that's my classroom) and our year-long excursion into the formidable math jungle begins.

"All aboard!"

We travel full-steam ahead, learning the basics of math, and soon we approach the first milestone event of high school: homecoming. I connect the homecoming theme chosen for the week with an appropriate math lesson. When they chose "Medieval Times" as their homecoming theme, I used the Geometer's Sketch Pad to help my students construct a Gothic arch. By exploring a website, they learned that Gothic arches are integral to Paris's Notre Dame Cathedral. Most of my students had only a limited familiarity with the intricacies of the cathedral, "Hey, this looks like the church in *The Hunchback of Notre Dame*," some noted.

I am relatively certain they were referring to the animated version of that classic tale, but at least their interest was piqued. I brought a Puzz3D model of the Notre Dame Cathedral to school to familiarize the students with its architecture. My students were quite interested in the arches, but they were amazed when they saw the cathedral's cross from above! To better understand the arch, each student constructed a gothic arch using a compass and straightedge ruler. As an integrated class project, the students cut paper into very small pieces and made a three-foot Gothic-arch mosaic with our high school mascot, the bearcat, in the center. The student council actually used our mosaic as part of the homecoming dance decorations.

"Goooooo, Bearcats," they yelled upon seeing their work on display.

I learned that any theme could be incorporated into the math curriculum by simply employing forethought and encouraging creativity!

After homecoming, my students' interest sometimes wanes. During long winter months, sports are always on their minds, so I keep the Math Express going. Hence, in 2005, I created "MATHens 2005: Still Going for the Gold."

This project connected the golden rectangle from mathematics, the golden ratio from architecture, and the golden spiral in nature by using an Olympic theme. With scenes from the recent Olympics in Athens still fresh in my students' minds, this project explored the Fibonacci sequence (a sequence of numbers, named after an Italian mathematician), and the golden ratio (approximately 1.6180339) that was used in the design of the Parthenon in Greece. Students used pictures of the Parthenon to create a golden rectangle and set up a proportion to the dimensions of the Parthenon, observing the similarity. A scale model of the Parthenon was constructed with the scale determined by the material that the students decided to use for the columns.

After the Olympics, we switched trains and went down various tracks on extensive side trips. The study of ellipses imaginatively transported us to St. Petersburg, where we learned about Russian czars and the House of Fabergé. What better topic for a unit near Easter? When I added the exhilarating strains of Tchaikovsky to our classroom setting, they implored, "Do we have to listen to this?"

"Of course," I calmly explained, "Tchaikovsky is good for the mathematical mind."

We created our own mathematical version of the legendary Fabergé eggs, keeping to the rules of ellipses. Students cut ellipses from gilded wrapping paper and mounted them on poster board using glass gemstones as the two foci. A gold braid illustrated the constant distance from each focus to the ellipse and back to the other focus. While we viewed photographs, we talked about the czar of Russia commissioning the eggs and their current valuation. Based on the spirit of Fabergé, each student completed a finely decorated two-dimensional egg. We displayed them in my classroom as well as in the lobby of the school, alongside pictures of Fabergé eggs for everyone in the school to view and assimilate.

As we wended our way through the peaks and valleys of the school year on our imaginary train, I was heartened to see my passengers thrive in the orderliness and creativity of algebra and geometry. Chugging merrily along, my students, with keen perception, pointed out sights and landmarks that I hadn't even noticed. The fact that they were finding their own applications and observations let me know that it had been a worthwhile and educationally rich and rewarding adventure.

All educators have a beginning point and curriculum goals to follow. The shortest distance from Point A to Point B, however, is not always the best decision. As I learned from a legendary tennis player, Arthur Ashe, "Success is a journey, not a destination." ❧

Making the Cut

SUSAN MENKES

High School, Visual Fine Arts
Jericho, New York

Our lives can change in a split second. This pivotal moment can happen anywhere, anytime. It happens at home, in business, and it happens, of course, at school. The moment of change that I am referring to could have occurred anywhere, but what was about to happen would happen in my fifth-grade elementary school art classroom. Within a fleeting moment, two of my students' lives would be altered forever.

The incident occurred during my second year of teaching art at a small elementary school in a quiet middle-class neighborhood on Long Island. The children were good kids with involved parents. I combined my passion for art and my love for children to inspire my students to develop their creativity. As a relatively new teacher, I felt comfortable that things were going very well both inside and outside my classroom. The State Education Department was developing new Visual Arts Standards for New York, and they chose one of my lessons as an exemplary example of the development process. It felt very exciting to be recognized as "on the cutting edge of art education." What was about to happen inside my art room, however, would add new meaning to the term "cutting edge" for me.

The class was working quietly and intently on a Matisse-like paper collage while I offered encouragement. "What you want to do is, 'draw with scissors,'" I told them.

This phrase, coined by the famous artist Henri Matisse in his later years, embodied the stylistic approach I wanted my students to take. I held up some jewel-toned paper and modeled the smooth cutting technique that produced wavy organic shapes. My hands and the scissors moved up and down, across the paper like a roller coaster. As I finished my demonstration, I told them, "You see, you draw with scissors like this."

Oh, if I had only possessed the power of a roller-coaster ride operator, I could have suspended the action to follow. It wasn't murder, or anything as drastic as that, if that's what you're thinking, but what was about to happen was something that no teacher wants to happen during class, especially a second-year teacher.

Just moments before, I had been happily gliding across the floor, gloating about how well my students were working. Matisse would have been so proud. Wonderful shapes were being drawn with scissors and little hands were dancing across paper with those sharp edges. Everyone was drawing with scissors and creating works of art.

Well, almost everyone. I say almost everyone because in that one roller-coaster moment, out of the corner of my eye, I saw it happen and felt my stomach drop. David, sitting directly across the table from Jessica, opened his scissors wide, put them near Jessica's forehead, and with one quick move snapped the scissors shut. What had been hanging in front of Jessica's tilted face, tilted in concentration on her artwork, were her beautiful bangs, which now lay lifeless on the table in front of her. David had done the unthinkable: He had cut off her hair!

Stubble sprouted along the crown of Jessica's head where once-thick bangs had matched her glossy long hair. The fallen hair blanketed her collage. It was a tossup as to who in the class had the most horrified look, but I feel confident it was me. "*Aaah! Oh, nooo!*" screamed Jessica, as if she had been stabbed (and she might as well have been), as she ran out of the art room to the girls' restroom to find an unforgiving mirror. David sat solemnly still, eyes wide, instantly recognizing that he was in big trouble. He appeared to be in shock himself.

David had certainly added new meaning to "cutting," at least in a school context. He was a polite young man, an honor student, brought up by caring parents, a choirboy with a strict religious background who had never cut a class, let alone hair. Jessica, a future homecoming queen, was an unspoiled, sweet, and popular honor student, as well. And I, an art teacher with a good reputation to uphold, was faced with a situation that took a big chunk, so to speak, out of the productive teaching experience I had been so recently enjoying. This was no "cut-and-dry" act; Jessica had lost her hair. I felt certain a parent conference would quickly follow, perhaps jeopardizing my job!

Panicky thoughts flooded my mind. *What if those scissors had found her eyes? It happened so fast. I didn't have time to stop him.*

David and his parents, Jessica and her parents, and I met later that afternoon with the principal. We sat solemnly around the same table that had served as the "scene of the crime." I felt the sting of Jessica's embarrassment. She had her hair pulled back and tied neatly with a pretty bow, compensating for the cruel haircut that exposed her virgin forehead.

"Sorry," David said tersely.

"Why did you do this?" the principal demanded.

"Sorry," was all David could muster. Since David offered no explanation for his impulsive act, he was justifiably suspended for two weeks. But, of course, both students survived. Both students went on to sixth grade. Jessica, unfortunately, began sixth grade sans bangs. In fact, two years passed until her bangs fully grew out again. But more importantly, years later, when David was seventeen, the story came full circle.

Standing in line to order lunch at a popular lunch spot near the high school where I was then teaching, I looked up to find a six-foot-tall senior standing next to me. I would have recognized that face anywhere. "You're David, aren't you?" I asked the wholesome teenager.

"Mrs. Menkes!" he said, smiling, and then casually asked, "Remember Jessica, and when I cut off her hair?"

I had the wrinkles and the gray hair to prove I remembered, but I purposely avoided pointing this out. "I think I recall that unfortunate incident," I calmly responded.

"Well, I'm really sorry that it happened in your classroom. But, guess what?"

I gave him a quizzical look.

"I'm taking Jessica to the prom next week."

We both laughed! Not long after, I saw a picture of Jessica and David on the front page of the local newspaper identifying them as the "Prom Queen and Prom King." In the picture, Jessica and David stood on a float smiling and holding hands. Jessica had long, thick hair, with thick bangs flowing under her crown.

Years passed, and I didn't hear anything more from either one of the royal couple. That is, not until a few weeks ago when I opened my mailbox and discovered a large pearly white envelope, elegantly addressed to me. David and Jessica had mailed me a wedding invitation, along with a handwritten note from David. "It all started in your art class," he said. "Back in fifth grade, I had a crush on Jessica and didn't know how to show it or how to get her attention. Thank you for giving me the opportunity to truly apologize to her by marrying her."

I read David's note and the wedding invitation again and again. Then, as I finally put them back in the envelope, I noticed something else was in the envelope as well—a lock of Jessica's thick, dark hair. ৩৩

I Teach Because of Baby Lions

SUE STINSON

Elementary, Wellness and Sports, Physical Education
Overland Park, Kansas

Being an elementary school teacher has its challenges. Being an elementary school physical education teacher has even more. You don't have a classroom to call your own, unless you have a gym, which is taken over for every possible school function; and you don't have a mind of your own, which is taken over by every possible thought process of the little children constantly surrounding you. As an example:

Last week I had something removed from my face, and no, it was not my nose. Now you may not find that last statement all that funny, but believe me when I tell you, my elementary kids found it *hilarious*. And when they saw a Scooby Doo bandage on my face, of course their inquiring little minds took flight. "What happened, Mrs. Stinson? Why do you have a bandage on your nose?" And then, virtually in unison, "Where's your nose, Mrs. Stinson?"

My theory: They want to know how you got a bandage so that they can decide if what you did would be worth having a bandage of their own. If you have ever considered becoming an elementary school teacher, especially an elementary school physical education teacher, then the following story will help you prepare. Of course, it's not true. What fun would that be?

So I say . . . "Well, you see, my mommy took me to the zoo, and the baby lion was sleeping. I couldn't see him real well, so I asked my mommy (small children think everybody's mommy is the same age as their own), if I could lean over the railing to see the baby lion better."

"My mommy said, 'No, that would not be safe.' (This is a reinforcement of lessons learned in school, of course.) I think she said something about why the railing was there, but I wasn't listening."

At this point, the little ones agreed that my mommy was right and heartily recommended that I should always listen to my mommy. Meanwhile, the bigger kids rolled their eyes and said, "Here she goes again."

"Sooo," I resumed, "when my mommy wasn't looking, I leaned way over and got sooooo close to the baby lion I could feel how soft he was." (The little ones gasped, the older ones snickered.) "And when I touched him, he started to wake up, and when he stretched, his claws accidentally scratched me, and that's why I have the bandage."

As the little ones stared at me wide-eyed, I wrapped up my fairy tale with a sweeping moral. "All I can say is that I am so glad it was just a baby lion, and from now on I will *always* do what my mommy tells me."

My little munchkins once again agreed that we all should always listen to our mommy because mommy knows what is best for us, and the older ones said, "You're lying."

To which I replied, "No, it was not 'my lion' it was the 'zoo's lion.'"

They just stared at me and shook their heads, and then they looked at each other and shook their heads again.

But this is why I teach: Because it's fun and because every day you have an opportunity to instill a valuable lesson about life!

Not long after, while I still had the bandage on my nose, our school celebrated Valentine's Day. I became the self-appointed official "Party Checker," which meant I got to visit the classrooms to see which class had the best treats.

I began in the first-grade classroom. They were still opening cards, but they gave me a bag of Valentine's cards.

Before I slipped away, I overheard Devin tell his mom, "Look what happened to Mrs. Stinson, the baby lion at the zoo scratched her."

"She was bad, she didn't listen to her mommy," Ashley informed her mom.

Many kids piped in, "You should always listen to your mommy."

Many moms looked at me with bewildered, yet thankful faces. I gave their party a B.

On to third grade, where they only had one cookie, and I had to get it myself, but it was very yummy, and my first cookie of the day. One mom stopped me on my way out, "What's this I heard about a lion at the zoo?" She hadn't heard that there was a new baby lion. She also didn't know lions were born in the wintertime, but she was planning on going this weekend with the kids to check it out because they kept asking about it. Time to move on! I gave their party a B-.

In the second-grade classroom, I scored three cookies, many sticky handfuls of those heart things (which I gave to my student teacher), but no brownies were left. The kids were engrossed in a game of bingo, using the heart things to cover the numbers. One dad caught my eye and said, "I heard about the lion at the zoo. I also heard that you didn't listen to your mommy. Tsk, tsk, tsk."

"What lion?" another mom asked.

Moms and dads and kids all started talking about the lion and some of them pointed at my nose. I distracted them by winning bingo! As my prize, I got to leave the room—permanently! The teacher ushered me out. I didn't get a brownie, but thanks to their three-cookie generosity, I gave their party an A-.

I then rushed upstairs to the fifth-grade classroom. Now these kids knew how to play the game. I walked in the door and my plate was immediately brought to me (bonus point). They already had it made up for me (another bonus point). Two boys promised to be my valentine, and I even got a hug (yes, from a fifth-grade boy).

"Hey, Mrs. Stinson, did you see how *big* that brownie was that we gave you?" Kids are never too shy to point these things out.

"Yeah," I said, "I love big brownies. And because of your generosity (I like to use *big* words around them; it impresses them so), I gave *you* an A+. How about that?"

They seemed impressed.

Once again, a mom stopped me on my way out, asking, "What happened to your face?"

Many groans could be heard in the room, and I thought I heard someone say, "Oh brother, here we go."

So, I gladly told my story. The kids were begging the adults to stop asking questions, but we were having so much fun annoying the munchkins that we spent a good ten minutes talking about it. One kid took up a collection to keep me quiet and got eleven brownies donated, which were mine if I would just stop talking about the zoo and the lion. Eleven brownies—now that's bargaining power! I stopped talking. As I left, carrying my plateful of brownies, the kids took turns giving each other high-fives.

Now it was on to the kindergarten, the new kids on the block. I had used the Halloween and holiday parties to teach them the Proper Party Rules According to Mrs. Stinson, and I couldn't wait to see how they fared on the last party of the year. They scored big with the food; I got three cookies right away (three with teeth marks), four kisses (the chocolate kind), something squishy and sticky (not real sure what it was in its original form), and a cupcake with no icing (I felt certain there was icing on it at one time.). I also received lots of hugs—kindergartners are great huggers!

While collecting my goodies (and hugs), I heard snippets of conversations going something like this:

"The lion . . ."

". . . and the zoo . . ."

". . . it was a baby with her mommy."

". . . she was a girl baby lion."

". . . and he was sleeping."

". . . her mommy told her . . ."

". . . the lion was soft and he was sleeping and he was a baby and . . ."

". . . and the railing . . ."

"... he woke up."

"... and it was a baby-boy lion and he ..."

"... but she didn't listen to her mommy and ..."

"... and he scratched her and ..."

"... but he really didn't bite her."

"... lions roar *loud* ... like this ... *ROOOOAAR!*"

And then the bell rang, which meant it was time to go home! I'm not sure what the parents were thinking, but the teachers said something like, "Just wait until we get you back."

I couldn't imagine what they meant. I gave their party an A.

You may think I overlooked one segment of our elementary student population, but you would be wrong. Going to a sixth-grade party means encountering skeptics and leaves one feeling as if one had endured self-inflicted torture, and even I don't subject myself to that.

By the end of the day, the kids, the parents, and the teachers were all yapping about the baby lion. (Of course, the latter group embellished, which was how those rumors started.)

Seriously, these exchanges provided some of the most joyous moments in my life. Working with kids, teaching kids, and letting their imaginations run wild makes me feel complete as a teacher. Of course, driving my coworkers crazy also helps, too.

I still have one more week to wear my bandage. I can't wait! ∾

PART V
Illuminations

The experience of teaching is influenced both in and out of the classroom. Teaching careers will be illuminated by many events over time, and each will impact a teacher's career from that point forward.

A Teacher Affects Eternity

JEFFREY THOMPSON

Elementary, Kindergarten
Fort Lewis, Washington

Kindergarten! Not a man's world, surely. What man in his right mind would want to take on such a challenge? This one.

That's right, I'm a male kindergarten teacher.

One of my most significant teaching events occurred with one of my students, named Johnny, during my first year of teaching kindergarten. I had been an integrated arts specialist for a number of years, instructing thousands of elementary students in music and visual arts, but I had always wanted a class to call my own. I wasn't satisfied with fifty minutes of contact with students each week, and felt I could make a stronger impact if I could focus on my own group of children. When I learned that a kindergarten position had become available within my building, I jumped at the chance. Many of my colleagues thought I was crazy to take on five-year-olds. Some described kindergarten as "glorified day care." Being a male teacher in the elementary school system was unusual enough, but teaching kindergarten, well surely, they thought, I had lost my mind.

In fact, I had thought very seriously about becoming a kindergarten teacher, and came to the conclusion that I could make a difference by developing and creating my own methods and materials, immersing the children in thematic learning, and raising current academic kindergarten expectations. I had a dream.

I designed "center time" to be an authentic experience for my students. My kindergarteners would become marine biologists, paleontologists, astronauts, botanists, and more. Each center would incorporate strong reading, writing, and mathematic connections, where the children could apply their skills in real-life situations. Students would have no idea how hard they were working as they applied themselves and developed their expertise. My students would leave my half-day kindergarten as strong readers, writers, and fearless scholars. I would shift the kindergarten paradigm and change attitudes. I feverishly worked throughout the summer planning my creative thematic units and building props and academic aids for my new students.

It was August, and I had just finished setting up my classroom for the first theme of the year when I heard a knock at my classroom door. Two young parents, holding the hands of a five-year-old boy, stood before me. The woman smiled and introduced herself and her son, Johnny. She told me that she was happy to hear that the school had a male kindergarten teacher because our other school was located on a military base, and most fathers were currently serving multiple, year-long deployments in Iraq. "I have been anxious to meet you, Mr. Thompson. I wanted the opportunity to speak with you before the school year begins," she said.

I invited Johnny to explore the room while his parents and I sat down to chat.

Johnny was taller than most kindergarteners, with sandy-brown curly hair, bright blue eyes, and a beautiful smile. I noticed that he didn't make eye contact and that he quickly settled himself in the math center where he silently explored the manipulatives (items the kids use with their hands to learn). One by one, Johnny used them to form a large pile on the floor. I was surprised that he didn't seem to notice my ocean-themed classroom, featuring a two-man, yellow submarine in an underwater world, with frolicking dolphins, seaweed swaying in the current, and a giant jellyfish. The room was ablaze with color, awakening all senses, but Johnny seemed oblivious to it.

Johnny's parents recognized that I was confused by their son's reaction (or lack thereof). Johnny's mom explained, "Johnny is autistic. We are very concerned about him being placed in your room." As her eyes traveled around the room, she added, "Your room is so visually stimulating that we don't think Johnny will be able to concentrate or behave here. We also don't think that he will be able to handle the general education curriculum. We're considering requesting that Johnny be placed in a self-contained classroom, but wanted to meet and talk with you before we made our final decision."

At the time, more than 30 percent of the school's students were medically or developmentally special needs students, so I was used to teaching children of all abilities as a music and art specialist; but I, too, had concerns about this child's placement in my kindergarten classroom. I had to ask myself some tough questions. Would the room be too visually distracting to Johnny? Would he be able to understand the curriculum? Would he be able to make friends?

Johnny's parents' concerns were valid, as were mine. We also had to face the questions all teachers have about all students. Will this child succeed? How far could I push this child's learning? Should I accept the parent's expectations for their child, or challenge them to raise their standards? Would the parents participate in their child's learning?

After a lengthy conversation, I could sense that Johnny's parents were committed to doing anything necessary to help their child succeed. They assured me that they would work with Johnny at home, and do whatever was necessary to help him. I took a deep breath and decided to follow my heart. I pointed to a sign above my door, which read "Mr. T's Learning Lab." "I want this 'lab' to be a place where we take risks. Johnny deserves a chance to succeed, but we will have to work together as a team. I will send extra assignments home for you to work on with Johnny, and we will all need to support Johnny as he adjusts to his new learning environment. Then, we'll see what happens and evaluate his progress down the road."

His parents agreed. On the first day of school, Johnny spoke with no one. He seemed content to sit at his table, coloring with only a green crayon. He couldn't, or wouldn't, sit on the carpet for calendar and reading lessons. He showed no interest in music or center time, when students worked together at creative, hands-on centers. Luckily, his mother had forewarned me that he might not distinguish between his father and me, so I didn't recoil when he called me Daddy. I asked the other kindergartners to help Johnny in the classroom. At the end of that first day, I worried that we had made a mistake. However, I had accepted the challenge, and had agreed with his parents that we would not give up easily. I had promised to give this my heart and soul.

Throughout the first few weeks, Johnny remained detached, yet seemed happy in his own world. I slowly began to explore opportunities to integrate Johnny with his peers, encouraging him to sit with his fellow students on the carpet for longer and longer periods of time. I also encouraged him to make eye contact with his teacher and his peers. As I discovered activities that Johnny preferred, rather than allow Johnny to quietly retreat to his centers, I engaged him by asking questions and offering him choices that required him to verbally answer me before he could engage in his favorite activities. I also designed activities that would compel Johnny to work as a teammate in small groups.

Johnny's classmates were remarkably patient and supportive, encouraging him every step of the way. I continued to work with him on his emergent attention span and slowly won more and more eye contact from him. I developed a close working relationship with Johnny and his mother, who was true to her word and kept her end of the bargain through regular teacher-parent contact and lots of help at home.

Gradually, Johnny became more aware of his peers and began to develop friendships, some he considered to be best friends. He was able to participate on the carpet for calendar and math, and with extra help at home, mastered his letter identification and sound demonstration lessons, all of which helped him become a member of the class. After the first month of kindergarten, Johnny became excited about school and couldn't wait to get into the classroom.

He slowly transformed into a wonderful student who interacted with both his teacher and his friends. He did well in his academics, and he began exhibiting changes that could be seen. Most notably, he abandoned his single green crayon and colored with every hue Crayola had to offer. Center time became his favorite activity, because he could develop his social skills as he learned about our themes. Johnny also began to read.

Teachers and administrators are required to prepare Individual Education Plans (IEP) for all special needs students. An IEP delineates specific educational goals and strategies to help the student become a successful learner. In May, at Johnny's IEP meeting, his parents informed me that they would soon be leaving the military and moving east to be closer to their family. His parents and I spoke of his transformation and the synergy that formed between teacher and parent. We talked about our mutual fears that Johnny wouldn't succeed, and about putting our faith in each other and following our hearts. In eight short months, Johnny's metamorphosis had been astounding. I was sad to hear that the student I had been so apprehensive about coming into my classroom would soon be leaving.

Johnny's mother told me that he talked about me all the time, and often talked about all the things he was learning in my classroom. She added, "Johnny tells me that he dreams about you and center time. One of the side effects of Johnny's autism is that he has a very vivid and long-lasting memory. I'm confident he will never forget his experiences with you and this classroom."

The feeling was mutual. Johnny had demonstrated incredible progress; his classmates had learned patience and understanding; and his parents now envisioned a brighter future for their son.

As Johnny walked out the door on his last day of school, he turned around, walked up to me, looked me straight in the eye, smiled, and gave me a hug, saying, "I will miss you, Mr. T."

With tears in my eyes, I hugged him back and said, "Johnny, I will miss you too!"

Henry Brooks Adams once wrote, "A teacher affects eternity . . . he can never tell where his influence stops." The same can be said for students. I had created a dream environment in which I hoped someone like Johnny would enjoy school, connect with those around him, and learn. Together, Johnny, his parents, my students, and I played an important role in transforming Johnny into a student who interacted with his peers, his teacher, and the world. Johnny and I developed a strong connection, and the lessons learned from recognizing the privilege of having Johnny in my classroom, taking a risk, and following my heart will stay with me for the rest of my life. ॐ

Gonna Draw

GAIL KREHER

High School, Special Needs, Literature and Journalism
Alpharetta, Georgia

When I went back to school to become a teacher, I envisioned a cheerful classroom filled with eager, bright children. Imagine my surprise when my first assignment was teaching learning disabled, mildly mentally handicapped, and behavior-disordered fourth graders, mostly from the lower socioeconomic scale. Because I had not had any training with special needs students, I felt completely unprepared. I had been worried about lesson plans, but now I worried about finding appropriate materials and developing effective individual strategies for my students.

Early on, Shawn became a challenge. Shawn spent most of his time drawing in the margin of his spelling paper when he was supposed to be studying the word families I had created for him. One day I tried to engage him in conversation. "So, what will you do for a living when fourth grade is history, and you are all grown-up?"

"Gonna draw," he mumbled.

"What kind of pictures . . . with pencils or paints?" Shawn merely glanced at me and continued drawing. Shawn seemed sad, and I really wanted to draw out a response. "Will you draw cartoon super heroes? Puppies? Horses?"

Shawn slowly lifted his eyes to meet mine, sighed wearily, and laid down his pencil. "Gonna draw. Like my daddy and my granddaddy."

"Oh!" I said, excitedly. "You live in a family of artists!"

Shawn squinted his green eyes, shook his head as if to say I didn't have the sense of a rabbit, and said, "Stay home. The mailman comes. Then he leaves. Then we go to the bank, and then get stuff at the store. Gonna *draw*."

I was still confused, but later it dawned on me that he was describing a sequence of events: The mailman comes, they go to the bank, and they get to buy something. I suddenly realized that he was telling me what happened when their welfare checks arrived. Clearly, Shawn and I faced a cultural divide, and it was my job to find a way to build a bridge between us that would breach that divide.

After weeks of pondering this dilemma, I came up with an idea: I would create a game called Friday Shopping at the Country Store. That night, I dumped the contents of my various junk drawers onto my bed and collected anything and everything that my students might find interesting: perfume samples, old beads, key chains, scarves, handbags, and castaway toys. When I brought them into school, the children were curious. I explained that they could earn points throughout the week and then use the points to shop on Fridays.

Most of the students were elated and crowded around to preview the treasures. Surprisingly, however, Shawn did not participate. Even though I invited him to join us, he seemed disinterested. His body language stated, *what's in it for me?* If he paid any attention, it was by looking askance, watching from his seat, preferring not to be part of the event.

I will admit that the first week was a little crazy. Counting and distributing the points proved overwhelming; but the children absolutely loved it, so I quickly found a way to make it work. The game definitely energized my students. They worked harder to complete their work on time and paid more attention to accuracy. For every task they successfully completed, I added points to their point cards, which they shoved into their pockets, desks, and change purses.

During the second week, Shawn gradually showed signs that he wanted to participate. He made an effort to increase his speed on classroom assignments, and, for the first time, turned in homework. Even if his papers were grubby and wrinkled, his work was accurate and complete. He soon earned extra points, and I felt increasingly optimistic that we would eventually connect.

Then, on Thursday of the third week, we had a breakthrough. It was one of those moments a teacher lives for and always remembers. Shawn slowly circled the table where the items on sale at the country store were displayed; and then he circled it again, carefully eyeing the goods.

The next day, he grudgingly held out his point card. "Gimme the flashlight," he said.

I probably grinned, recognizing that I had finally found a way to motivate Shawn. "You can double your points if you'll sit in the hot seat," I said. The hot seat was another game we played. Once students agreed to sit in it, I would quiz them on background information, such as the months of the year, the seasons, and the names of U.S. presidents. If they answered correctly, they could double their points.

Shawn looked at the flashlight, and then he looked at me. "Okay," he said.

Not surprisingly, he nailed every question I fired at him.

We were both excited: Shawn because he was doubling his points and me because I felt as if we were truly building a relational bridge between us. The deep chasm now felt manageable. We had connected.

I soon created other learning games and activities designed to make learning fun. We wrote a newspaper, put on a play, continued to shop every Friday, and learned a lot.

Just this past year, Shawn's mom spotted me in the supermarket and called out to me, "You're Mrs. Kreher, aren't you?"

"I am," I answered, smiling.

"I have to tell you about Shawn," she said, pausing to breathe. "He ended up going to technical school and graduated! He found a good job and worked so hard they recently promoted him to be a supervisor in charge of eleven people! Shawn loved your class, and everything you did to help him made all the difference."

Later, I pondered this and realized that I was the one who should feel grateful. After all, Shawn had taught me a useful teaching method. I had arrived at my creative solution by answering his simple question, "What's in it for me?"

By offering the children meaningful rewards, I motivated them to work harder, but I became the real winner in our game. What I gained was far more substantial than trinkets; I learned the joy of helping students awaken to their fabulous potential, especially when they faced unusual challenges. Helping students enjoy the learning process and helping students develop self-esteem proved extremely rewarding.

Today, I teach in a private school. All of my students have individual special needs, and I still have to figure out what is important for each one of them, what will best motivate them to discard bad habits and surrender old disappointments and limited expectations. Thanks to Shawn, I learned I'm "Gonna Draw." I'm going to draw on each child's individual needs so I can respond and plan appropriately to make a difference in their lives. ∾

What Does It Take to Teach?

GLENN LID

High School, Science
Maywood, Illinois

I teach high school in a tough environment, and within that hostile environment I teach a challenging course: science. On the other hand, tough environments are good for my other line of work, which is coaching. Tough kids make good wrestlers, but it's still a hostile environment. Tough environments and challenging classes sometimes don't go together as well as tough environments and tough sports, but effective teachers can make even the toughest learning situations a great place for students to prepare themselves for success.

The key to helping students from tough environments succeed lies in creating relationships with them. For example, Justin, a young man in my advanced placement chemistry class and a starter on the wrestling team, confided to the coaches that while he slept, his drug-addicted mother had been taking money he hid in his socks to help pay for her drug habits. Justin wanted to go into the armed services, but he also wanted to go to college right away. I knew what a tremendous student he was and, being the academician I am, I was hoping for the college route.

"Justin," I told him, "I think we can get you into college."

I worked very hard with Justin and the uncle who was taking care of him to make college a credible option for him. He performed well on the ACT, received a full scholarship from the University of Illinois, received his degree in nuclear engineering, and now works as an electrical engineer for Commonwealth Edison. I invite Justin to return each year on career day in hopes his story will motivate my students.

Working with young adults like these often means going over and above what many teachers are willing to do. I took one of my wrestlers, who was also a baseball player and a chemistry student, mountain climbing in Colorado for two summers because I recognized his love for the outdoors. Two of the math teachers and I took one of our former graduates and her family to dinner when she graduated from medical school this year. My wife and I have established a book scholarship at Elmhurst College for students who attend Elmhurst after graduating from the high school where I teach. I give out a pin of a Mickey Mouse hand, with the thumb pointing up, to twenty of my outstanding students at the end of the year who have earned the Power of the Pin Award.

I often read excerpts from Frederick Douglass's works at the beginning of the class period to let students know that learning how to read and getting an education is what set him free. I also read inspirational poems from Maya Angelou, Marie Currie, Helen Keller, and Kyle Menard. Following up on kids in a tough environment also means early wakeup calls. I call my athletes at the crack of dawn to make sure they are on their way to school. I make every attempt to convey to students and the community that I really do care about them, and that I am not there just to teach chemistry, but to help them succeed. To teach them about persistence, I share stories about previous students and the struggles they have overcome.

Providing structure is also another important ingredient to overcoming impediments. All teachers have to deal with interruptions, accepting new students into their environment at any point and dealing with tardy students on a daily basis. Establishing a structure helps your students learn to adhere to a logical set of rules. Believe it or not, they actually appreciate the discipline. Students know they cannot interrupt a demonstration once it has begun; they know where to pick up their assignment; they have to wait at the door until I say they can sit down; and if they break the rules, they know that they have lost five points from their participation grade.

I also require all students and their parents to sign a lab safety contract. This helps students understand the consequences for misbehavior in the lab. We take time to review materials and look toward future classes so that students are well aware of what will be on exams and what activities and assignments are coming up. Vulgar language is a big problem in the halls in our tough environment, and even though I emphasize that it's unacceptable in my room, it still happens. As the instructor, I take time out to explain to my students why cursing is not acceptable, why being tardy works against them, and why arguing with one another is not productive.

Structure also builds mutual understanding and respect. To make it work, I make time to explain to students why I am disciplining them for certain behaviors. Maintaining structure is like traversing a swift river; you cannot be absolute, but must allow room for creative decisions that will get you safely to the other side. Discipline must always be positive in nature, recognize certain limits, and not be so repressive that it drives students back to the streets. When disciplinary actions are needed, we try to learn from them.

How does someone like me compete with Tiger Woods? How do some of my students compete in baseball, wrestling, or chemistry with students in surrounding communities who enter high school more academically prepared? As the famous golfer Ben Hogan once said, "The harder I work the luckier I get."

Through hard work, my students begin to see the learning curve really isn't a curve at all—it's a vertical line. With hard work, they begin to believe they can become champions both on and off the playing field, and in the classroom. Even if my students don't go on to further their education, I want them to leave my class with fond memories, to know how chemistry affects their lives, and with the feeling they can, as Maya Angelou says, "Let nothing dim the light that shines from within."

I urge my students not to allow their environment to dim the positive energy inside of them. They face formidable obstacles and they know it. Together, we help each other navigate our tough environment; together, we help each other succeed. Teaching is one of the greatest professions in the world because teachers have the greatest gifts of all to give: knowledge, confidence, opportunities, and happiness. ✑

Teaching Gems

BRIGITTE TENNIS

Middle School, Humanities
Redmond, Washington

Diamonds, rubies, sapphires, pearls, and emeralds—those are the gems that I have collected over a long teaching career. Now, don't get me wrong, every day in the classroom is not a "diamond day" because learning is not always pretty! There are math problems to puzzle over, grammar exercises to slog through, and hormonal ups and downs that resemble the ever-bouncing movement of a yo-yo. But, within the everyday work of striving to instill the fire of learning in our young people, small gems show themselves in tiny, but flashy sparkles—the challenge is, how observant are you—the teacher? Can you catch those glimmers of gemstone in the classroom?

During my first year of teaching, twenty-six years ago, I had a zeal that could not be matched by Superwoman! I planned exciting experiments, collected papers with a flourish, and challenged my second-grade class so much that we finished the entire curriculum by the beginning of April. What was I to do then? We still had two months of school left to go! I decided to empower my students, by asking *them* what they'd like to learn.

They looked at me, and then at each other. At first, they were confused. Second graders are not often offered such an opportunity. Those students lit up with joy, and after much animated discussion, they decided they wanted to put on a play. "Mrs. Tennis," they said in unison, "not a play. We want a *musical*."

And not just any musical—these students wanted to perform *The Wizard of Oz*!

Triumphantly, my little second-grade gems looked to me, their teacher, to direct them. Of course, they wanted to do all the songs and all the scenes with no parts watered-down for their age. However, I had never directed a musical before. I wondered nervously where I would get the money for costumes. And props. And what about the script?

"Please, can we do the play, Mrs. Tennis?" they asked, using those ever-effective puppy-dog eyes.

They had worked so hard all year long; how could I let those little enthusiastic faces down? My task, daunting as it was, was laid out before me—so I buckled down and wrote a script myself, and then we began the task of learning how to put together a stage show from the bottom up. The students rehearsed their lines and practiced singing to my piano accompaniment (I was about sick of "Somewhere Over the Rainbow" by the performance). We hand-painted scenery on king-sized bed sheets donated by parents, worked with parent-helpers to create costumes, and attempted to master the difficult art of stage choreography every moment the gym was not in use for PE classes.

On performance day, 250 parents and grandparents packed the gym, all armed with cameras to record the momentous event.

For the next two hours, we wowed them with winged monkeys wearing panty hose over their heads; a Tin Man coifed with an aluminum-wrapped silver funnel and spray-painted boxes fitted around his body; a melting Wicked Witch who cleverly disappeared under the stage at the appropriate time; and Dorothy, played perfectly by a student named Amy. As I watched those children sing and dance their way across the stage, I saw quite a few sapphires and diamonds twinkling!

About ten years ago, I was invited to Amy's bridal shower—and the theme was "Somewhere Over the Rainbow!" In the living room, guests watched video of my budding second-grade actors and actresses, marveling at their accomplishment. At the end of the tape, the leading lady (and bride-to-be) informed everyone that she planned to become a teacher, thanks to me. I was amazed that this young lady had gained so much from me in such a brief time of her life! This "emerald" helped me realize that what teachers give to students really does have an impact and, sometimes, it really does last a lifetime.

• • •

Another year, I had a group of sixth graders who really needed to acquire empathy and consideration for others. In hopes of creating a climate of compassion, I inquired at our local senior center to see if some elderly people might be willing to visit with us once a month. After much reassuring, ten distinguished men and women in their eighties agreed to visit my classroom.

When the two age groups met for the first time, everyone seemed nervous—young and old alike. I could almost hear the thoughts bouncing around the room. *Will she like me? What if he can't hear me? Will they laugh at me?* But within minutes, everyone engaged in a Picasso-type art activity, cleverly designed to require teamwork. Fears soon faded into giggles and light conversation. Over time, bonds of friendship and caring developed. One day in early February, the students called a class meeting to inform me that they thought two of the seniors liked each other. They asked me to arrange an art activity where those two seniors could work together so they might "fall in love."

What little matchmakers! At their beckoning, I created several opportunities for those seniors and their little charges to work together, and when the two senior citizens announced to the class that they were getting married that spring, my students cheered and clapped with knowing nods of "I told you so" discreetly cast in my direction.

The students and I were invited to the summer wedding, and as the sun shone brightly, gems both young and old flashed brilliantly in its rays. Their sparkle showed me that love *does* conquer all—even kids can see that!

• • •

About thirteen years ago, my mother suffered a heart attack and died suddenly. At the time, I was teaching sixth grade. My students were aware of what had happened and expressed their heartfelt sorrow. When I returned from bereavement leave,

I had difficulty focusing on which concept I was teaching in reading, what page we were on in math, or who I needed to call on because this or that student had not answered a question yet.

A few days before Mother's Day, I cried in class, though I tried valiantly not to. A sixth-grade girl, Samantha, got out of her seat and courageously walked straight up to me at the front of the room. Bold as brass, she said in a calm but confident voice, "Mrs. Tennis, I know it hurts. I lost my little brother to Sudden Infant Death Syndrome two years ago." Samantha looked up at me and smiled. "It's okay to cry. And if you want to cry on my shoulder, I am here for you." And, you know, I did just that.

What did I learn from this? People rise to become what is needed. I needed a mother figure, and there she was—in a twelve-year-old girl. She was a priceless diamond that sparkled when I most needed it, and I have never forgotten that gesture of kindness and compassion.

The whole experience taught me to live my life by the motto, *Carpe Diem*—seize the day. Today, I seize the day by cherishing every moment I have on this earth and by being a "gem" to anyone who needs it.

• • •

And finally, there's Andrew.

The middle school years can be especially challenging for parents, teachers, and students. Hormones have the kids bouncing around the classroom and newly found independence gains them the confidence to say, "I know all of this! You can't teach me anything!" Heels dig in, mouths clam up, and "attitude" can flick its barbed tail at a classroom teacher quicker than a stingray! Yes, that's middle school. Many people wonder where the sparkling gems are during these intense years of development, but I can assure you that they are still there. You may have to dig a little deeper and look a little harder to uncover them, but they are there!

On the first day of school, Andrew stomped into my seventh-grade classroom wearing shiny black army boots, camouflage gear, and a fez jammed on top of his head. He plopped himself down at a desk and within the first five minutes of my welcome, shouted, "I don't need this d*m* stuff!" He then shoved his desk out of the way, stomped across the floor as loudly as he could, and slammed the door on his way out. Needless to say, the rest of the class was stunned. They silently waited to see what I would do. Gathering all of my courage, I calmly walked out into the hall and gently closed the door.

Andrew hadn't gone far and immediately challenged me. "Aren't you gonna leave the door open so they can hear you yelling at me?"

I explained that I did not yell, and that I would rather discuss whatever was bothering him so I could teach him all the cool things that seventh grade had to offer. Andrew looked at me quizzically and gave a curt nod. I told him I would love to chat with him after school (he was surprised I was not calling his parents) and invited him to come back into the classroom if he felt like it.

I walked back into the classroom, leaving the door ajar for him to follow, and picked up where I had left off with my first-day welcome. Andrew did not come in to the classroom again that day, but he did show up after school. He confessed that things were kind of rough at home and admitted that he wanted to learn, but he did not want to do "a bunch of mindless work" as he had done in the past. I could see that the sparkle was there. I assured Andrew that I would make things interesting and challenging for him, and that I wanted him to be in my class.

Over the next three weeks, the whole class pulsated with the desire to help Andrew succeed, and Andrew helped the class—although he probably didn't realize it. Most of the students wanted to be in Andrew's group, and they encouraged him to participate, which he did. This young man's intensity became energizing, leading him to come up with innovative ideas that other students had never even thought about. I worked hard to plan interesting, meaningful, and hands-on learning experiences. We performed chemical experiments, setting off minor explosions that thrilled the students. We studied Roman gladiators; marveled at the beauty of the inner parts of a flower; and read the ancient tale *Beowulf* together. Within a month, a new Andrew was emerging. I knew we had turned the corner when, one morning as I was writing the schedule on the chalkboard, I heard a deep commanding voice say, "Dude, we're doing history and science today! Hurry up! Sit down, guys!"

Although I had my back to the class, I knew it was Andrew's voice, and I smiled inside. Andrew had found the "fire of learning," and I had found a pearl under that hard shell.

A number of years later, I saw Andrew at the local theater, and he excitedly told me that he was going to France to be a chef! An amazing turnaround from that first day in seventh grade, but we must always remember that even the most tightly closed oyster may have a pearl developing inside. As a teacher, it is my job to nurture that gem and bring it out from inside its tough exterior.

So when people ask me why I am a teacher, I just smile and tell them of the treasured gems that I have collected over the years. I have a whole chest of beautiful sparkling jewels, and that's enough for me! ∾

Lessons from the Classroom

CINDY ROSSER

Elementary, Kindergarten and 1st Grade
Anchorage, Alaska

The only sound in my first-grade classroom came from the scrape of a pencil across paper. All the children had been excused for recess, except one, who sat at his desk, gripping his pencil, nervously glancing up to the board, and then quickly trying to duplicate the symbols on the paper before their shapes evaporated in his mind. I watched him struggle until I couldn't bear it anymore, and then rose to go sit by him. My supervisor, sitting in the back of the room, cleared her throat, glared at me, and slowly shook her head, mouthing, "*No!*"

I sat back down and waited. It seemed like hours passed before the little boy finally lay his head down on his arms. "I no do it," he said, sobbing. "I no can do more."

Ignoring my supervisor's glare, I walked over and put my arm around him. "Let me see your paper," I said softly, slipping the paper out from under his arms.

The poem he attempted to copy from the board contained many mistakes and was obviously incomplete. Teachers don't like receiving unfinished work, but supervisors detest it. Still, my heart went out to him. "Alban," I said softly, "you can go outside for recess now and finish this later." Alban wiped his face on his sleeve and hurried out of the room before my instruction could be vetoed.

"Ms. Rosser," my supervisor said slowly, "you are much too easy on these students. You should have made him finish the assignment."

I hesitated before speaking. She was there, after all, to judge my teaching abilities. It seemed prudent to weigh my response carefully. "Alban is an ESL (English as a Second Language) student," I explained. "He couldn't even read the words he was copying."

My supervisor let out a short breath. "This was a handwriting assignment. He was practicing his formation of the letters, not comprehension. Unfortunately, he will assume that you'll be an easy mark when he wants to get out of doing hard coursework."

Unfortunately, a teacher often has to play this game with administrators. "He is only in first grade and just learning to speak English," I reiterated calmly. "I doubt that he is planning ways to avoid his class work."

Although an unpleasant moment, that interchange forever altered the way I work with children. I became the determined one. I began taking intensive courses on how to work with younger children, and started asking questions of my own. What stimulates their learning? What kinds of activities are necessary for them to come to understand the world around them? What role do I play in their lives? How do I create an environment in the classroom that is conducive to their learning? How did

I need to change? How can I help my kids while still appearing to conform to the dictates of supervisors?

I had always been involved with drama and music (I minored in Fine Arts), but I really had not applied those talents to the classroom. I decided to use music to help my ESL students learn English. We sang our way through the days of the week and the months of the year.

Alban seemed to be able to memorize better to music. His oral language improved, and his writing skills increased. His family even invited me to their home to talk to them about programs that were available that would help his parents learn English. Wow, getting parents involved . . . now *that* would impress any supervisor.

I helped organize school-wide activities that promoted cultural awareness and parental involvement. We began to learn about our students' rich customs and cultures. Parents shared their homeland experiences in class presentations. They helped set up hall displays and assisted their children with classroom assignments. With the help of Alban's parents, we organized a special cultural awareness day. His parents brought in treasured items and books and created a museum-like display. They stayed to teach his classmates phrases in their language and teach us native dances and songs. When I later adapted one of their folktales into a play, Alban's parents helped gather traditional clothing for the characters to wear.

We made "passports" and studied geography in preparation for an imaginary trip to Alban's homeland. When we "traveled" via our classroom airlines to his country, his parents and relatives greeted us. The children feasted on a luscious potluck with specialty dishes provided by the community. Later, we performed our folktale and dances for the entire school with Alban as one of the central characters. The audience of teachers and students clapped and cheered and yelled and screamed (as elementary students invariably will do). Instead of feeling like an outsider, Alban became an instant celebrity. He experienced the joy of being from a special culture with enchanting lessons to share. He beamed with pride throughout the whole day, and smiled often from then on. School became a place where he and his family felt welcomed. I had, along with my students, created a safe place for them.

I became more actively involved in our community and encouraged Alban's parents to do the same. I chaired several committees focusing on school-wide programs to involve students and their parents in cultural programs. I researched legends from different cultures and wrote plays and musicals for the rest of our student body to perform for the community. My classroom and our school became like a family, bound by many cultures.

Over the past twenty years, my teaching methods have evolved. I discovered that this is necessary not only to keep up with the times, but to make my time in the classroom energetic and fresh for my students. I still use lots of poetry, but not for mindless copying projects. Our poems are funny or teach a concept of science or touch our lives with insights. In fact, we now write our own poems.

I have often reflected on that moment with Alban and the supervisor. I feel so grateful that he touched my heart, and that I found the courage to stand my ground. Little did I realize at the time how much I would grow as a teacher when I decided to change things for the better. Many years later, I met Alban's brother at a conference. He was the student aide helping set up computers. He told me that Alban had stayed in school, learned English, graduated from high school, and was considering which colleges he might attend. "You know, my family really thinks that Alban was pretty lucky to have been in the ESL learning center with you," he said. "Those three years really helped."

I told him that I had been the lucky one. Alban was the one who had taught me. He taught me that teachers should always seek the joy that is discovered when one finds methods that will fill their students with a desire to learn. He taught me that supervisors sometimes need to allow the teacher to decide what is best for the students they know so well, regardless of what is written in the lesson plans. He taught me that learning from each other can have an amazing impact on both the teacher and the student, changing both of their worlds forever. ∾

What Makes a School Daddy?

BRIAN FREEMAN

Elementary, Kindergarten
Red Springs, North Carolina

Some teachers are called "Mr.," some are called "Ms.," and some are called names that cannot be discussed in polite settings. The latter, by the way, are often the most effective teachers because they make their students *think*. As for me, well, my students usually call me "the School Daddy." If you think that is an unusual nickname, you would have to understand that I've had an unusual career.

Many moons ago, when I was attending college at UNC-Pembroke in Pembroke, North Carolina, I wanted a career that would make me rich and famous. Doesn't everyone dream of making big bucks and seeing their name in lights? I did, and I hope you did, too.

I planned to become a success—and a star—by majoring in broadcast journalism. I anticipated fully that I would be able to accomplish my *Lifestyles of the Rich and Famous* dream with a career in television news. That dream, as I soon discovered, would turn into a nightmare.

I graduated with a degree in broadcast journalism and assumed I was ready to go. Unfortunately, not a single network banged on my door and zero jobs materialized. After a year, I had no job lined up and no prospects. I felt certain I had enough rejection letters to win a spot in the *Guinness Book of World Records*—a college graduate's worst nightmare come true. I had to face the facts: I was bankrupt and desperate for money. I was even on the verge of selling my plasma. If I hadn't been afraid of needles, I would have been first in the donor line. Instead, I decided to do something I never thought I would do: I signed up as a substitute teacher. This prospect was also terrifying, but it seemed less physically painful. Little did I know that pain comes in many forms and that the ability of students to torture teachers could be excruciatingly painful. Children have an ability to predatorily sense the vulnerability of a substitute teacher.

My torture commenced immediately. A charming villain, disguised as a principal, lured me into accepting a long-term substitute assignment and sentenced me to teach twenty-nine fourth graders (untamed and unsettling misfits) housed in a small trailer. Sardines, it would seem, had more room.

Of course, I greeted them cheerfully. "Hi kids, I'm Mr. Freeman. I'm your new teacher, and we're going to have *lots* of fun!!!" I wanted to set the right tone.

Apparently, so did they, saying in unison, "Who cares, Mr. Freeman?" and then laughing "ha-ha-ha-ha-ha-ha."

Oh, this was going to be . . . fun?

After meeting my students, I suspected their normal teacher wasn't on sick leave, as explained to me, but rather on a much-needed vacation. Clearly, I thought, that teacher knew something I didn't. Donating plasma was back on the table.

One student, aptly named Genesis, as in the genesis of problems, abused me on a daily basis, and really seemed to enjoy it. The daredevil in him made him want to torture me; alas, the daredevil in me accepted the challenge. I needed a way to win over these students, and quickly realized that I had to begin at the beginning, just like the biblical Genesis.

The lesson-plan book provided by the "sick" teacher resembled an ancient witches-brew cookbook with wrinkly, tea-stained pages. I could have sworn I saw a drop of plasma on the first page (or maybe it was a tearstain). As I dusted it off, I noticed it had more pages than an encyclopedia. To be completely honest, I had never read an encyclopedia from cover to cover, so the chances of me reading and following the lesson plans left behind by someone else were slim to none. Even if I were so inclined, every time I attempted to use the lesson plans, the students let me know they were bored with their textbook and its accompanying worksheets. I had to make a plan of my own, not rely on someone else (if I was going to survive).

Luckily, I had a capacity for creativity and an ability to have fun. I relied on my knack of looking at things differently as a tool to make my teaching fun and innovative, which I thought would make it more interesting for me—and my students. I climbed on top of a student's desk to sing, dance, and even perform rap songs. I created a math lesson called the Multiplication Soul Train, in which I rapped multiplication facts and multiplication questions. The students with the right answers got to dance down the center of the "Soul Train line." All of a sudden, students not only became attentive, they became mesmerized—by math! More importantly, their academic achievement and behavior began to improve. Even Genesis became more angelic.

As we progressed together, I developed more creative ideas. I found a costume that allowed me to become a skeleton, which I used to teach students about "Dem Bones." I even found some bone-shaped candy to go with the theme.

In the end, the transformations I saw in these students inspired me, and changed my life. I definitely experienced pride in what I had accomplished, and, once rested, I realized that I had truly found a meaningful profession, a place where I could make a difference. I surrendered my dream of becoming a wealthy TV newscaster, and returned to UNC-Pembroke to acquire my teaching certification. My goal became finding ways to utilize my creative and humorous talents to make a difference in children's lives. I had, quite simply, fallen in love with the light that goes on in children's eyes when they learn a new concept or feel proud of their accomplishments. That priceless twinkle is the reason I teach.

Irony? After earning my teaching certification, I returned to the same matchbox-sized classroom to begin my teaching career. My new fourth graders were studying family lineage. A well-bred student named Kathryn was leading a discussion about her family, when a less-advantaged student named Chason said, "I don't have no daddy."

Without missing a beat I said, "Yes you do, Chason. You have a daddy. I am your daddy at school."

"That's right," she said, smiling. "You are my daddy . . . my School Daddy."

The nickname stuck, and of all titles ascribed to me, "School Daddy" is the one I am most proud to bear. If being the School Daddy allows me to help my low-income and minority students overcome the many obstacles they face to become successful,

I am happy to do it. This School Daddy teaches for all the students who are low achievers or have behavioral issues. This School Daddy teaches for all the students who live in poverty or in single-parent homes or with grandparents as their caretakers. This School Daddy also teaches for all the students who come from middle- and upper-income homes with two parents, who may or may not be happy, but still have their issues.

What makes a school daddy? A school daddy believes that all children, regardless of color, ethnicity, income, or achievement levels deserve a quality education. A school daddy believes students should have a chance to discover, in a creative and nurturing environment, that they need to love themselves, and love learning. But most of all, a school daddy is a teacher who, when the teaching gets rough, continues to strive for excellence, sticks with it, makes a difference . . . and keeps all his plasma right where it belongs—in his body, giving him strength to meet the new day. ❧

THUMZ ZUP

JOE UNDERWOOD, EDD, NBCT

High School, Television Production and Moviemaking
Miami, Florida

After being selected as a Disney Teacher Award Honoree, I found myself in the company of fantastic teachers, and wondered how I was ever so lucky to be chosen. Little did I realize how soon these wonderful people would make a difference in my life.

Our "class" of thirty-nine Honorees (that's what we are called) assembled at Disneyland in July 2004 for an amazing week of parties, parades, and a gala befitting rock stars and actors—twenty-eight of our class have contributed to the book you are now reading. What a thrill! But there's more. One reason becoming a Disney Teacher Award Honoree is so meaningful is that we bond as a group and gather throughout the year for professional development sessions. This professional development began in Anaheim and was to continue several months later, in October, at Disney World in Orlando. Unfortunately, bad things can—and did—happen between Anaheim and Orlando, between July and October.

All the Honorees anxiously looked forward to our Orlando gathering. How important was this trip to me? I had rearranged my football-officiating schedule, which was extremely out of character. This I never did; I loved football season. In fact, I had officiated five football games in one week, when I woke up one Sunday morning suffering stomach cramps. I dismissed this discomfort, but my wife Nancy, who handles these types of situations much better than I do, insisted on taking me to the emergency room. Seventeen hours and three CT scans later, I found myself on a gurney, being wheeled from ER to OR for surgery. A lump had been discovered in my colon. After removing it, the surgeon said, "We got it all."

After a week of hospitalization, I finally convinced one of my doctors, whom I kept referring to as Dr. Discharge, to let me go home. Just before signing out, an oncologist named Dr. Fu explained that I had cancer—non-Hodgkin's lymphoma—and told me I would have to undergo chemotherapy treatments. She emphasized that some compromises would have to be made.

"I can't," I told her. "I have too many things to do."

"You will," she replied, "or you won't have to worry about what you have to do."

Everything changed. I was going to be out of school for some time (totally unacceptable); I had to immediately give up officiating football, not for a week, but for an entire season (a devastating loss); and my upcoming trip to be with my fellow Disney Teacher Award Honorees was in jeopardy (and only two weeks away).

Concerned fellow Honorees began calling to ask how I was doing, if there was anything they could do to help. Even though I was still recovering from surgery, since my chemo treatments were still a few weeks away, Dr. Fu told me I could travel to Orlando for our sessions, if I felt well enough. I let my fellow Honorees know I *was* going to be in Orlando.

That Thursday, I had an appointment for a bone-marrow test. After a mild sedative, a needle was inserted into the bone in my hip and a sample of tissue was withdrawn. Okay, not so bad. Wait, now we will switch sides and do it all over again. So, Dr. Fu punctured my other hip and proceeded to take another tissue sample. While my bone marrow was sent to a lab for testing, I was sent home to rest. I needed it for my long drive coming up in less than twenty-four hours.

Luckily, driving in Florida is relatively easy compared to other states. It is all flat and straight. But, if you have recently had surgery on your stomach and needles poked through your hipbones, I can assure you it is not especially comfortable. I felt like I had been beaten up. Other than that, my drive was great.

Since first becoming a Disney Teacher Award Honoree, I had been looking for something to symbolize my accomplishment, but I could never find exactly what I wanted. When I arrived in Orlando and checked into Disney's Contemporary Hotel, however, I finally found what I was looking for among hundreds of pins. On a rectangular field of red, bordered by a gold edge, Mickey Mouse's hand offered a thumbs-up sign. Perfect! I was positive I would overcome this cancer thing, so I wanted a way to inspire others to feel equally positive. Also, one of my fondest memories growing up is of my father giving me a thumbs up whenever I did something that pleased him. This pin summed it all up; I wore it every day during our professional development.

Our reunion and learning experience proved wonderfully enriching. We began our week of activities by writing the name of a student we believed in on a piece of paper and putting it away. As our meetings progressed over the next few days, a couple of my colleagues would point to my thumbs-up pin and remark how cool they thought it was.

None of us looked forward to our professional (and personal) development session ending, and Saturday came sooner than anyone wanted. All our principals were there, plus the Disney staff—about eighty people altogether.

As we stood outside our hotel in a large circle for our final encounter, we spoke about each student whose name we had written down on the first day. Progressing around our circle, students' names were stated and our individual and collective belief in them kept pouring forth. As our circle of belief neared its end, Brigitte Tennis, one of my fellow Honorees, read a collective statement that said, in effect, "Joe, we believe in you and are behind you in your fight against cancer. We know you will overcome this obstacle because of your positive attitude, and we love you." Everyone was staring at me as she continued, "Honorees, please take out your pins." At this point, everyone pulled out a thumbs-up pin and held it up. "We are going to wear these pins every day until you go into remission," she said.

My heartfelt emotions made it literally difficult to breathe. I could not believe that this diverse group of wonderful educators would express such a moving dedication to one person—to me. Every one of them stayed to give me a hug. I couldn't wait to get to my room to call Nancy and let her know that my life had just been changed forever.

But the story of the thumbs-up pin did not stop there. These teachers, and others, took its meaning to whole new levels. Glenn Lid, a fellow Honoree, chemistry teacher, and wrestling coach from Illinois, told me that his students had asked about the pin when he returned from our time in Orlando, so he told them my story. Several weeks later, I received a package in the mail. Inside was a picture of Glenn with one of his classes, about twenty-five students. In the photo, each student was smiling broadly and holding or wearing a thumbs-up pin. One student held a sign that said, "Mr. Underwood, we believe in you. Thumbs Up!"

Glenn also began bestowing a Power of the Pin award at the end of the school year to one of his students who had overcome adversity. He and I have toyed with the idea of bringing our wrestling teams together for a "Thumz Zup" invitational.

Meanwhile, over in Kansas, fellow Honoree Jason Larison's wife, Sarah, was training to run in a marathon, something she had never done before. Sarah contacted me and gave me the surprise of a lifetime. The marathon for leukemia and lymphoma research would be held in California, and Sarah wanted to run the race in my name as an Honored Survivor. She asked if she could wear "THE PIN" while she was running. This request came when I was in the middle of chemotherapy, without a single hair left on my body (I just thought that it made me a sexy bald guy), so it was extra special to think someone in Kansas wanted to run, in my name, out in California.

"Of course," I told her. "I would be thrilled."

I sent her a pin that day. I also let all my fellow Honorees, football officials, and friends know about the marathon. We raised $4,000 for Sarah, and for leukemia/lymphoma research. I have listed this event on my resume as one of the highest honors I have ever received.

The Power of the Pin did not run its course after only twenty-six miles, either. Another Honoree, Warren Phillips, was invited

to appear on the television show *Who Wants to Be a Millionaire?*
Warren wore his pin on his lapel and swore it helped him win.
Maestra and fellow Honoree Carol Boyer recently gave her pin
to a friend diagnosed with breast cancer. Our entire group let
Carol's friend know that the Power of the Pin is very strong.
Other Honorees continue to wear their pin on their jackets and
ID cards at school and continue to support me in many ways.

When we all got back together for our final professional
development in October of "our year" out in Anaheim, I arrived
at the Grand Californian hotel at Disneyland and was greeted
by all of the other Honorees. I had completed chemotherapy,
but was still sans hair. It made me so happy to see everyone and
to see that every single one of them was wearing their pin.

I am told that many people ask the Honorees about those
pins, and now there are several hundred people, including students, wearing a thumbs-up pin as a reminder that this pin
helped someone overcome a fight against cancer—that positive
thinking and the loving support of others can make a significant
difference in many lives.

I have not yet completely overcome my battle with non-
Hodgkin's lymphoma. I am not cured, but I am in full remission. Dr. Fu remains very optimistic. I continue to wear my
pin every day (Nancy knows I still wear it because it has created little holes in every shirt I own). That pin, and the support
of my Disney Teachers, has helped me get to this stage in the
remission process and to keep a championship outlook toward
winning the battle against cancer. Nothing in my professional
life has felt more magical.

Thumz Zup! ❧

The Last Goodbye

JANEY LAYMAN

High School, Information Science and Business
Alverton, Pennsylvania

As our yearlong experience as the Disney Teacher Award
Honorees for 2004 came to a close, we teachers said our last
goodbyes, many with tears in our eyes. Walking down the
hallway in the Grand Californian Hotel in Anaheim, California,
at 1:00 A.M., I felt a shiver as I looked down upon the quiet,
massive lobby below. I paused to gaze at the place where it all
started, where we came together to discuss the importance of
teaching, and how we strive to make a difference in our students'
lives, the place where laughter rang, friendships began, and our
lives changed. I cherished the excitement, the growth, and the
magic that had taken place—a year of amazing adventures that
will be with me forever. It was time to go home, time to find a
way, somehow, to bottle this positive energy, this desire to be
highly effective teachers, and this joy of teaching, so we could
pass it on.

Every year I write my high school seniors a goodbye letter
that's posted on our online magazine.

As I stood lingering a little longer, staring at the beauty of the hotel lobby below, I thought about my seniors and how they came together, and soon, how they would proceed. Often, they don't realize how much their lives change upon graduation. They, too, would soon have this feeling that "it's over." They would walk out of a familiar place where they had shared so many smiles one last time. I thought about them and about these teachers, and reflected upon our shared transition. Here's the letter I sent to them, and hereby offer my colleagues, both those who had the privilege of being honored and those who work tirelessly to teach our children well.

To my seniors,

Please take one more look around before you leave. School is an awesome place, whether you realize it right now or not. There are so many memories wrapped up here that it will be hard to capture all of them in just one moment. Remember the lessons learned, the hope your teachers have for you, and the possibilities that await you. I hope you will smile as you look back on graduation night, just as I am looking back now. Take a snapshot in your mind of this time of your life and reflect upon it often. Walk down the hall and out to the commons one more time. Cherish the excitement, the growth, and the magic that's happened in each of your lives during the past twelve years. Think about the difference you have made in someone's life, and the difference they have made in yours. Tell your friends and family how thankful you are for them. Tell your teachers, too, because believe it or not, they really will miss you. Then keep in your heart my wish for you: Life is an amazing adventure. Make it the ride of your life! ∾*

About the Authors

The Disney Teacher Awards was an outreach program of the Walt Disney Company from 1989 through 2006, recognizing creative teachers who actively engaged students in the learning process. Since its inception, almost 600 teachers from across the United States have been honored. For additional information, please visit *www.DisneyOutreach.com.*

Each of the authors in this anthology were Disney Teacher Award Honorees in the class of 2004. Additional biographical information follows and is provided in alphabetical order.

CINDY LOU AILLAUD

Delta Junction, Alaska

Cindy encouraged her elementary students to develop a life-long love for health and movement, despite living in rural Alaska, where subzero temperatures are common. Her students—and their families—participated in an annual walking challenge, even though it was 20 below! Cindy began her career as a physical education teacher in 1998, and previously taught as a regular classroom teacher and a special educator. She authored and photographed *Recess at 20 Below*. In 1993, Cindy became Delta/Greely Education Association Teacher of the Year. In 2000, she was named a Fulbright Memorial Scholar. In 2005, she was named the Conoco-Phillips Local Fitness Champion. Cindy has served as co-president of her local education association for six years. She chairs the Steering and Rules Committee at the National Education Association state delegate assembly, and served as president of the Alaska Association of Health, Physical Education, Recreation, and Dance. She was awarded membership on the *USA Today* 2006 All-American Teacher Team and received a gubernatorial appointment to the Professional Teaching Practices Commission. Cindy is looking forward to meeting many women around the country in her role as a National Trainer for the NEA-Women's Leadership Cadre. Having recently retired from the Delta/Greely School District, Cindy is now self-employed and visits schools across the country, sharing *Recess at 20 Below* and encouraging students to write their own stories.

CAROL BOYER

Elma, Washington

Carol is a literacy specialist at Educational Service District 113 in Olympia, Washington. One of Carol's first classrooms was a thirty-five-foot motor home parked on a ranch in Washington's Yakima Valley. This "little school on wheels" emphasized education for children of migrant farm workers. Carol was named a Toyota Tapestry award winner in Science and Literacy in 2003, an Intel Teach to the Future Master Teacher in 2003, and a Disney Teacher Award Honoree in 2004.

BRIAN FREEMAN

Red Springs, North Carolina

Brian is a National Board Certified kindergarten teacher. He has dedicated his fifteen-year teaching career to helping low-income and minority children. Living up to his nickname of School Daddy, Brian does whatever it takes to motivate his students. He will sing, rap, dance, or even dress up as Little Red Riding Hood's granny to teach them valuable lessons. Brian was named the North Carolina Wal-Mart Teacher of the Year, winning an $11,000 grant for his school. In 2004, in addition to being a Disney Teacher Award Honoree, he became the National Second Grade Teacher of the Year by Staff Development for Educators. *USA Today* twice named him one of the top-forty teachers in the nation. He traveled over 50,000 miles representing the 3.2 million members of the National Education Association as the recipient of the prestigious NEA Foundation Teaching Excellence Award, for which he received a personal cash prize of $35,000. Brian partnered with Leapfrog Learning Products and served as one of their national educational spokespeople. Dozens of television and radio stations across the country have interviewed Brian. In addition, Brian has been profiled in *Woman's Day* and *Good Housekeeping* magazines. Outside the classroom, he has served as president, vice president, treasurer, and district president for his local and state teacher association (NCAE). Brian also served a four-year term on his local town council. He is an active member of the North Carolina Professional Teaching Standards Commission and Chair of the North Carolina Foundation for Public School Children. He used a portion of the NEA Foundation prize money to establish an endowed scholarship for an elementary education major at his alma mater, UNC-Pembroke. Brian has written a book of inspiration for parents and educators and hopes to have it published in the near future.

LIZ GALLEGO

Dallas, Texas

Liz teaches dance with a focus on community building and personal empowerment through culture and the arts. Through her leadership, students have set meaningful goals and taken responsibility for their learning. A veteran teacher of thirty-five years, she credits her seventeen years of experience with the Dallas Public Schools for bringing depth to her craft. Today, she teaches dance part time at Mountain View College in Dallas and has a private dance-therapy practice. She continues her involvement in cultural dance as president of the Texas Association for Hispanic Dance and Culture. Liz was named to the Committee to Revise the National Standards for Dance by the National Dance Association (NDA) in 2003, and was nominated as Artist/Scholar of the Year by NDA in 2008. In 2002, she was the first dance teacher featured on the website of the Center for Educator Development in the Fine Arts.

JULIE HARRIS

San Diego, California

Julie has thirty years of experience in public education, working with elementary-age students, college students, fellow educators, and, of course, parents. In her time as a first-through-sixth-grade educator, Julie has taught gifted students, special education students, and English language learners. Her teaching spans a wide range of school settings, including five years in South Central Los Angeles. Julie served a two-year appointment as Distinguished Teacher in Residence in the College of Education, California State University, San Marcos. Additionally, at Turtleback Elementary School, Julie developed a parent education program called the Smart Cookie Club, a partnership between home and school. She opened an adult learning resource center at Turtleback, to be used for both parents and teachers. Julie recently opened the latest elementary school in her district, Willow Grove, having served on the Leadership Team for the planning of that site. Julie is also a volunteer for the KPBS Public Radio Reading Service, and has a claim to fame as a contestant champion on television's *Jeopardy!* Julie and her husband, Gary Neiger, reside in San Diego, California.

SALLY AUSTIN HUNDLEY

Waynesville, North Carolina

Sally has over fourteen years of experience teaching in the Southern Appalachian Mountains of Western North Carolina. Along with her teammate, Mellie Hamilton Cope (Micky), she created a progressive program for at-risk eighth graders in her middle school. Sally received her bachelor of arts degree in Social Studies Education and Political Science from the University of North Carolina at Chapel Hill and a master's degree in Educational Media in 2004. She is currently a doctoral student in Educational Leadership. Sally is a National Board Certified Teacher in Early Adolescent Mathematics. She has worked on projects with Apple Computers, the National Board for Professional Teaching Standards, the International Society for Technology in Education, Hewlett-Packard, and the AT&T Foundation.

Although these projects keep her running, Mrs. Hundley spends most of her time chasing after her own elementary-age children, Sarah and Cub. Her accomplishments in education are dedicated to her husband, Ron, who refused to let her leave the profession during those early, difficult moments of teaching and who has given pep talks too numerous to count.

DEB HURST

Austin, Texas

Deb is a kindergarten teacher at Mills Elementary in Austin. Her unique classroom includes children with disabilities and English language learners. Deb started her career teaching deaf and hearing-impaired children across central Iowa. After moving to Texas she used her special education background to start an innovative inclusion classroom for children with special needs. Her classroom won a Texas Promising Practice award and became a model for inclusion and developmentally appropriate practices. After completing her master's degree at the University of Texas, she received certification for English as a Second Language. Her classroom often has as many as eleven different languages being spoken at one time. Deb excels in building classroom community and involving the cultures of each child into her lessons. Deb was selected Teacher of the Year at two elementary schools and a semi-finalist twice in her district. She is a National Board Certified teacher and trains new teachers in her district and throughout her region. She has written curriculum at the district and state level and has presented at national and international conferences. Deb was a finalist for the HEB Excellence in Teaching Award for lifetime achievement. Teaching for 33 years, Deb measures her success by how she can make a difference in each child's life and to instill a love for learning that will last for the rest of their lives. Deb lives in Buda, Texas, with her husband Greg. She is especially proud of her son Michael, daughter Amy, and her two grandsons, Hunter and Jake.

HECTOR IBARRA, PHD

Iowa City, Iowa

Hector has been a middle-school science teacher for more than thirty years. A unique person whose collaboration with teachers extends beyond his school to district, state, national, and international levels, he realizes the importance of providing opportunities for his students, other teachers, businesses, and community members. Hector received his PhD from the University of Iowa and has visited Japan on numerous occasions to continue his role as a Fulbright Scholar. In 2005, he was named Wal-Mart National Teacher of the Year. He is also a member of the National Teachers Hall of Fame in Emporia, Kansas. Hector's students have participated in many prestigious national science competitions, where they are often found in the winner's circle.

TAMMY HAGGERTY JONES

Sauk Village, Illinois

Tammy has served for six years as a Field Ambassador, writing exhibit curriculum and providing student outreach programs, for the Field Museum in Chicago. In 2007, Tammy participated in an archaeological dig with paleontologists from the Field Museum, during which they unearthed a 12,000-year-old mastodon. She has also served on the Teacher Advisory Board at the John G. Shedd Aquarium since 2002, where she also writes curriculum and provides student outreach programs. In 2008, Tammy was named Teacher of the Year by the Kids in Need Foundation, and also joined a Shedd Aquarium team of marine biologists and educators on a Teacher Field Experience spent snorkeling in the Bahamas. In 2005, Tammy traveled to Japan with the Fulbright Memorial Fund Teacher Program. In 2006, she received the National-Louis University's R.E.A.C.H. Lifetime Achievement Award. She has been a guest speaker at Roosevelt University, Governors State University, and Chicago State University. She is a contributor in *The Best Practices for Teacher Leadership: What Award-Winning Teachers Do for Their Professional Learning Communities*, published by Corwin Press. In 2006, Tammy received a scholarship from the Chicago Alumni Club to participate in the Excellence in Teaching conference at Notre Dame University.

GAIL KREHER

Alpharetta, Georgia

Gail teaches language arts and journalism to college-bound high school students who struggle with attention deficit and learning disorders, including Asperger's, Tourette's Syndrome, and Obsessive Compulsive Disorder (OCD). Gail believes in her school's philosophy, "Success in School, Success in Life." For more than sixteen years, she has lovingly pushed her special needs students to realize their incredible potential. As one example, her small staff of journalism students turns out a web-based thirty-page newspaper every three weeks. Many of her students attend college and return to say, "Thank you for giving me strategies to do what I thought I couldn't do." Gail holds a MEd in Special Education from North Georgia College and State University, and a BA in English from Syracuse University. Prior to discovering her true calling as a teacher, Gail worked as a TV weathercaster for ten years. Known professionally as Gail Janus, she performed on nightly news programs, hosted various specials, and worked as a commercial radio and TV commercial talent in Atlanta; New Haven, Connecticut; and Worcester, Massachusetts. She currently teaches at Mill Springs Academy in Alpharetta.

JASON KUHLMAN

Central Point, Oregon

Jason exemplifies the creative and highly motivated professional teacher that any principal would want to hire. His classroom is a warm and welcoming room with constant activities, creative instruction, and caring but firm guidelines. As a first- and second-grade teacher, Jason has captured both the art and science of teaching. In 2005, the government of Japan honored Jason by presenting him with a Fulbright Memorial Fund scholarship. Jason was one of three finalists for his state's 2006 Presidential Excellence Award for Teaching Science. He lives in southern Oregon with his wife Aimee; their two children, Levi and Olivia; and their two Chihuahuas, Pépe and Skip. His professional goals are to become an elementary principal and publish some of the stories he makes up for his students.

JASON M. LARISON

Holton, Kansas

Jason has been the Agriculture Education Teacher and FFA Advisor at Holton High School for fourteen years. He graduated from Kansas State University in 1995 with a bachelor of science degree in Agriculture. In 1999, he completed his master's degree in Secondary Education, and his teaching license is in Agriculture Education and Biology. In 1999, the National Association of Agriculture Educators (NAAE) recognized Jason as an Outstanding Young Member. In 2002, Jason was a finalist for the National FFA Agriscience Teacher of the Year. Under Jason's supervision, the Holton FFA Chapter was ranked number one in Kansas for five years. From 2005–2008, he served as a teacher representative on the National FFA Board of Directors. Jason, his wife Sarah, and daughter Lora Anne live in Holton.

CASEY LAROSA

Montclair, New Jersey

Casey is in her eighteenth year of teaching. She currently teaches middle school social studies in Montclair. Teaching became her second career and one of the joys of her life. She loves touching the lives of young people every day and strives to offer them hope for the future. Casey's husband, Jerry, and her two children, Chelsea and Vermond, remain her staunchest supporters. According to her four siblings—Keith, Kevin, Wendy, and Janice—on the day she passed her teaching exam, she reportedly danced around the yard singing, "I'm a teacher, I'm a teacher, I'm a teacher. . . ."

JANEY LAYMAN

Alverton, Pennsylvania

Janey uses her background in corporate America and as a former professor to bring real-life skills to her computer science, entrepreneurship, and business classes. For her, the world is the classroom, and the possibilities for student learning adventures are limited only by their imaginations. She is best known for bringing her own version of *The Apprentice* to the high school classroom, by having her students manage real-life projects as close as possible to what happens on the television show. Janey believes that service-learning is an integral part of any curriculum. She created and chairs the Wal-Mart & Wendy's Frosty Open Golf Tournament for the Dave Thomas Foundation for Adoption and the Children's Miracle Network, where her students manage and run the entire tournament, with all proceeds donated to the charities. In 2003, Janey was named a Radio Shack National Teacher Award Winner. In 2005, she was selected as a *USA Today* All-Star Teacher, and in 2007 traveled to Japan as an education ambassador through the Japan Fulbright Memorial Fund. Janey is a member of Phi Beta Lambda honorary, and has been listed in *Who's Who in Teaching* for several years. In addition to teaching, she is a travel agent, and was selected by Royal Caribbean as one of the top finalists for Godmother on *Liberty of the Seas*.

GLENN LID

Maywood, Illinois

Glenn has been teaching science, honors chemistry, and advanced-placement chemistry at Proviso East High School in Maywood for more than twenty-five years. Glenn uses his creativity and his sense of humor to relate science to things in everyday life. Glenn thinks of his classes as *exocharmic*, a word created by a mentor. His mission is to exude as much positive energy, humor, creativity, and inspiration into his lessons as possible. His students enter Glenn's room knowing that they can succeed and that Glenn really cares about their future. Glenn graduated from Elmhurst College with highest honors in Biology and Physical Education, with a Chemistry minor. Glenn coaches wrestling and baseball. In 1986 and 1991, Glenn's wrestling teams won state championships, and his baseball teams have won regional and state titles, as well. In 1993, he received the Presidential Award in Science Instruction from the Illinois Science Teachers Association. In 2007, he earned the Teacher of Distinction Award from the Illinois Golden Apple Foundation, and the Davidson Award for excellence in chemistry instruction from the Chemical Industry Council of Illinois.

DANNY MAGRÁNS

Clarksville, Tennessee

Danny makes Spanish come to life at Clarksville High School, encouraging personal ownership in learning by having his students communicate with orphans in Mexico and other Latin cultures, as well as traveling to Spain and Mexico. Danny requires his students to apply higher-order thinking skills. He is the creator and sponsor of the HOPE Club (Helping Others Progress Everyday), whose mission is to raise money to help those in need. Danny and his students are listed in the 1999 and 2003 *Guinness Book of World Records* for the longest paperclip chain, which measured 20.44 miles. He and his students also biked across Tennessee in 2004 and 2005 to raise money for the American Diabetes Association. In 2005, Danny was selected as one of the K-Mart Teachers of the Year.

DARLENE MARTIN

Grafton, West Virginia

Darlene teaches Geometry, Algebra II, and Honors Algebra at Grafton High School. An innovative and imaginative math teacher, Darlene's commitment to excellence is second to none. In 1981, Darlene was named Grafton High School Teacher of the Year. In 1999, she was honored as a Milken Family Foundation National Educator, and in 2000, Darlene was the Grafton Wal-Mart Teacher of the Year. In 2007, Darlene received the Arch Coal Teacher Achievement Award. Through numerous mini-grants, Darlene continues integrating mathematics and art in her classroom to help enrich her students' lives.

SUSAN MENKES

Jericho, New York

Susan currently teaches art at Cantiague Elementary School in Jericho, and has been teaching art on Long Island for the past seventeen years. Her passion for art, as well as her love for children, sets the stage as she strives to make a difference in the lives of her students. In a true inclusion environment, Susan not only develops creativity, divergent thinking, and problem solving, but also fosters in her students a love and appreciation for art and art history. Her famous art-related magic tricks have earned her the nickname Mrs. Magic Menkes. Susan infuses the art of world cultures in her lessons to teach about respect, tolerance, and understanding differences. She continually seeks to design art projects that make learning about world cultures come alive. In 2006, Susan was one of twenty teachers from across the nation chosen to be on the *USA Today* All-Teacher Team. In 2000, Susan was the recipient of the New York State Art Educator of the Year Award/Long Island for professional excellence in the field of art education. In 2001, she received the Robert Rauschenberg Power of Art Award. In 2002, she was awarded Fulbright Memorial Fund Scholarships from Japan and the United States.

Susan is an active member of the Long Island Art Teachers Association. Her hobbies include painting in her studio, reading, and traveling. She has two children and three grandchildren and resides on Long Island with her husband, George.

WARREN PHILLIPS

Plymouth, Massachusetts

Warren is a dream come true for his seventh-grade students at Plymouth Community Intermediate School. Warren teaches Integrated Science, Service Learning, and TV Technology. Warren is known for his teaching methodology, his love for children, and for providing fantastical energy and fun. He calls his science environment "emotional learning," and infuses it with thematic demonstrations, songs, and stories that cement facts, ideas, and scientific concepts while creating unforgettable experiences for his students. In 2001, 2002, and 2003, Warren was a finalist for the Massachusetts Presidential Award in Secondary Science. In 2002, he received the Time for Kids/Chevrolet Excellence in Teaching Award. Warren has written and produced several CDs containing songs about science and learning entitled *Sing-A-Long Science*. In 2006, he was selected to the *USA Today* Teacher Team and also received a Presidential Service Award. He is a contributing author to the Prentice-Hall *Science Explorer* textbook series and the National Science Teacher Association's monograph series entitled *Exemplary Science in Grades 5–8*. In 2007, Warren was elected to the Massachusetts Science Teachers Hall of Fame. In 2008, he also received a fellowship for an Earthwatch Expedition to study elephants in Kenya. He is National Board (NBPTS) certified in Early Adolescent Science and maintains an informative website: *www.wphillips.com*.

CINDY ROSSER

Anchorage, Alaska

Cindy teaches second grade at Creekside Park Elementary School in Anchorage. In Cindy's second-grade family, the arts remain an integral part of the curriculum. Children are given the opportunity for expression and growth by participation in dance, art, theater, and music. Cindy believes children learn the many facets of a curriculum better when they are a creative part of the arts. Her children excel as they absorb new information and develop fluency of skills through a thoughtful mixture of imaginative play, repetition of skills, laughter, and fun. In 1999, Cindy was named the Phi Beta Kappa Golden Apple Award winner. In 2000, she was a presenter at the Alaska Science and Technology Conference, and the recipient of the ASD Technology Award for Integration.

Ms. Rosser has written over twenty plays and musicals based on units of study in science, social studies, and asset building that have been presented to thousands of school children, parents, and community members. From counting with animals on a farm to rapping with the Cohesion Brothers, juggling to the tunes of a circus or bringing traditional native stories to life, her students learn through music and dance. She shares her plays with other teachers so they can incorporate them into their curriculum as well.

SUE STINSON

Overland Park, Kansas

Sue is a teacher who possesses the extraordinary gift of being able to make each child believe in his or her own ability. Sue's love of her job and her students is palpable. Her colleagues are amazed by her ability to touch the lives of so many children and expect nothing in return. Sue is involved in many school activities, including the Teacher Walking Program and Fit the Deck All School Games. Outside of her school activities, she is a huge Boston Red Sox fan.

BRIGITTE TENNIS

Redmond, Washington

Brigitte is the founder and headmistress of Stella Schola Middle School in Redmond. The school is based on the principle that all students can learn, and that during the often-tumultuous middle school years, students need stability and structure without surrendering their wonder of learning. Brigitte feels that it is essential for teachers to demonstrate an excitement for learning and a healthy work ethic. Brigitte graduated from the University of Washington on an academic scholarship, completing her bachelor's degrees in Violin Performance and K–12 Education. She attained her master's equivalency in Education, and recently completed her National Board Certification as a nationally recognized professional teacher of excellence in English. In 2004, 2005, and 2006, Brigitte was a Jefferson Award Nominee at the Regional Level for Public Service. She is also a member of the National Latin Honor Society. In 2002, Brigitte received the Outstanding Educator Award for Dedication and Service from Rose Hill Junior High PTA. Since 1981, Brigitte has been teaching in the Lake Washington School District in Washington State and continues to serve as a mentor to new teachers in her school. She often performs violin recitals for retirement-home residents in the Seattle area, volunteers for the summer Special Olympics, and continues to support the greater Seattle area and the young women of Seattle as a former Miss Seafair, Queen of the Seas.

JEFFREY THOMPSON

Fort Lewis, Washington

Jeffrey teaches kindergarten at Evergreen Elementary School on the Fort Lewis U.S. Army Post. He has shifted focus from exposure to learning skills to mastery of reading and writing, and parent education and participation play key roles in his students' learning. Jeffrey's students leave kindergarten as strong readers, so they can spend less time in the future learning to read and can concentrate on reading to learn. Jeffrey has a bachelor's of Business Administration degree and a master's in Education, Curriculum, and Instruction. While his students are Jeffrey's priority, he also works with educators as a certified Critical Friends Group Coach and is a national motivational speaker. Jeffrey was selected by the Disney Teacher Class of 2004 as both the Outstanding Elementary Teacher and Disney Teacher of the Year and has represented the Class of 2004 throughout the nation. In 2005, he appeared in the first *Who Wants to Be a Millionaire* "Teachers Week." In 2006, he was awarded an ING Unsung Hero Award. The Butler-Cooley Excellence in Teaching Award and recognition as a *USA Today* All-Star Teacher were bestowed on Jeffrey in 2007.

JOE UNDERWOOD, EDD, NBCT

Miami, Florida

Joe is the Leading Learner of ARTEC, an Entertainment Technologies Academy at Miami High School. He has been teaching at Miami High since 1984, and in 1988 began developing his television-production classes into what has become a small learning community within the historic, 100-plus-year-old secondary school. Joe passionately believes that his students can succeed, which leads to the motto of the program: Real Experience for Real Careers. In 1998, his program was selected as one of nine VTECS Pilot programs from around the nation. The VTECS schools were a part of the United States Department of Education's sixteen Career Clusters, which incorporated national standards into the curriculum. Television students produce a live, student-run, ten-minute newscast daily throughout the school year at Miami High, and have been doing so since 1988. Through innovation and collaboration, Dr. Underwood's program has expanded to include courses in moviemaking and entertainment law. Joe has a bachelor's degree in Speech/Theatre from Tennessee Tech University (1975), Cookeville, Tennessee and a master's degree in Sports Medicine from the United States Sports Academy (1987) in Daphne, Alabama. He received his doctoral degree in Educational Leadership from Nova Southeastern University (2006). He is certified by the National Board for Professional Teaching Standards and by the National Athletic Trainers Association, and serves on the Governor's State Board of Athletic Training. He has been the athletic trainer for ten Miami High state basketball-championship teams since 1987. An avid football official for over twenty-two years, Joe serves as the president of the Greater Miami Athletic Conference Football Officials Association and is on the state Sports Officials Advisory Committee. Joe was selected as a *USA Today* All-Star Teacher, and in 2006, along with being named a local Wal-Mart Teacher of the Year, he was one of twenty teachers nationwide to participate in the Toyota International Teacher Program of study in the Galapagos Islands. In 2007, Joe was recognized by the prestigious College Board as one of six teachers nationally to receive the Bob Costas Writing Grant, and was one of five teachers nationwide to be inducted into the National Teachers Hall of Fame in Emporia, Kansas. Named as a Japan Fulbright Memorial Teacher in 2008, Joe spent three weeks as an educational ambassador in Japan. He is also an actor who has appeared in motion pictures as well as national and international television commercials. His wife, Nancy, is a veteran teacher at the elementary level. They enjoy traveling to the outer islands of the Bahamas with their daughter, Jolene, when time permits.

CLAUDE VALLE

Weston, Massachusetts

Claude has been teaching math at Weston Middle School for twenty years. A featured teacher on *Tokudane* (the Japanese version of *The Today Show*), getting kids engaged in learning is Claude's goal; i.e., he works hard to make math interesting, fun, varied, and connected. Claude believes that all people have the brainpower to do math; the key is unlocking that potential. Recipient of a Massachusetts Governor's citation for excellence in teaching, Claude has authored numerous articles on teaching and learning for several publications, has been a featured instructor in the Massachusetts Teachers Association's monthly magazine, and has spoken at two Weston High graduation ceremonies. He holds a BS in Mathematics, MS in Statistics, and a MEd in Middle School Education. In addition, Claude has coached high school swimming for twenty-five years. Named a 1997 EMSCA Meritorious Service Award winner, 2001 and 2008 Swimming Coach of the Year by the *Boston Globe*, and a 2002 AFLAC National Coach of the Year, Claude's 2007–2008 Weston High School team was undefeated, had eleven All-America qualifiers, and set five Massachusetts state swimming records on their way to the state team title. Outside the classroom, Claude enjoys time with his wife Jean (a preschool teacher), and their three children, C. J., David, and Katie.

PAM VAUGHAN

Camden, Arkansas

Pam is a biology teacher at Camden Fairview High School in Camden. In 2002, Pam was recognized as the National Space Club Space Educator of the Year and a Cornell CONTOUR Comet Challenge National Student-Teacher Team Winner. In 2003, she was the Arkansas Education Association Human Relations Award Winner. In 2005, she was named a member of the *USA Today* All Star Teaching Team. In 2007, she and her students were selected as NASA Phoenix Mars Lander Interns. In 2008, she was selected the National Biology Teachers Association Outstanding Biology Teacher for the state of Arkansas.

Her enthusiasm for NASA education programs has earned her the title NASA Teacher in Arkansas. She and her students have received national recognition for success in a variety of NASA educational programs. Pam received her National Board Certification in Science for Adolescence and Young Adults in 2005. She serves as an appointee to the Arkansas Governor's Council for the Education of the Gifted and Talented, and as a member of the Arkansas Science, Engineering, and Mathematics Coalition. She has traveled to Japan as an educational ambassador through the Japan Fulbright Memorial Fund. In her unique science classroom, some are writing a song, some are acting, some are building, some are calculating, and some are creating artwork. Students learn to draw on each other's strengths and learn to appreciate individual differences and contributions. On the first day in her classroom, Pam tells her students that she loves teaching and that in her class learning from mistakes is a goal, not a failure. Students are then invited to join the adventure.

DARRELL WOODS

North Canton, Ohio

Darrell is a physics teacher and cochairman for the science department at Hoover High School. His previous teaching experience includes nine years at Jackson High School, where he taught physics and mathematics; and seven years at St. Thomas Aquinas High School, where he taught physics, biology, general science, and calculus. He earned his Bachelor of Arts in biology from Walsh College in 1983 and his Master's in Science in comparative anatomy and immunology from the University of Akron in 1983. He holds an Ohio teaching certificate in comprehensive science and mathematics. In addition to his teaching, Darrell is extremely active in Teen Institute, a drug prevention and education organization, and has served as an advisor during the past fourteen years. Darrell is a National Board Certified Teacher in Science for Adolescence and Young Adults (renewed, 2008) and was honored in 2003 with the Presidential Award for Excellence in Mathematics and Science Teaching. He was also a finalist for the 2008 National Teachers Hall of Fame, a finalist for the 2007 Ohio Teacher of the Year, a member of the *USA Today* 2006 All USA Teacher Team, and a winner of the Great Lakes Science Center WOW Award (2003), Chevy Malibu Teaching Excellence Award (First Place 2001), and Ashland Oil Teacher Achievement Award (2000). He participated in the Inaugural 2002 Akron Global Polymer Academy Institute; participated in NASA's Educational Workshop for Mathematics, Science, and Technology (1995); and served on Governor Taft's Ohio Teacher Advisory Committee (2000–2001). Most recently,

Darrell was honored with the Walsh University 2008 Outstanding Alumni Award.

When not involved in school activities, Darrell and his wife Jacalyn are busy raising their three sons, Zachary, Joshua, and Benjamin, in the small community of North Canton, Ohio.

AIMEE YOUNG

Loudonville, Ohio

Aimee is in her seventeenth year of teaching high school English in Loudonville, where she has also been teaching Holocaust studies, an elective she created over the past eleven years. Aimee also teaches AP literature and composition, creative writing, writing for college, and studies in literature. She was recently chosen as a National Writing Project Fellow for 2008, and has been a Regional Museum Educator for the United States Holocaust Memorial Museum since 2005. Aimee has presented different aspects of educational issues surrounding the teaching of the Holocaust to a variety of audiences nationally, regionally, and within the state of Ohio. She has had lessons and articles published by the United States Holocaust Memorial Museum and *Teaching Tolerance Magazine* (in print and online), as well as for Beacon Press (online teacher's guide). Aimee is a mentor teacher for her school district and a member of the school district's Local Professional Development Committee. She and her husband Kenny have three children: Jerrica, Natalie, and Connor.